Merry Christmas 1998
from Dick & Pat

My
Mother
Played the
Piano

My Mother Played the Piano

More Tender Stories of Home
to Deepen Your Faith

JOHN WILLIAM SMITH

HOWARD®
PUBLISHING CO.

West Monroe, Louisiana

Our purpose at Howard Publishing is to:

- *Increase faith* in the hearts of growing Christians
- *Inspire holiness* in the lives of believers
- *Instill hope* in the hearts of struggling people everywhere

Because He's coming again!

Published by Howard Publishing Co., Inc.,
3117 North 7th Street, West Monroe, Louisiana 71291-2227

97 98 99 00 01 02 03 04 05 06   10 9 8 7 6 5 4 3 2

Library of Congress Cataloging-in-Publication Data
Smith, John William.
     My mother played the piano : more touching stories of home to
inspire and encourage the heart / John William Smith.
          p. cm.
     ISBN 1-878990-75-6
     1. Meditations. 2. Smith, John William.   I. Title.
BV4832.2.S5485 1997
242—dc21   97-4348
                                                                              CIP

Cover design by LinDee Loveland
Manuscript editing by Philis Boultinghouse
Illustrations by Tex Stephenson

Scripture references are from the following sources: the New International Version (NIV), © 1973, 1978, 1984 by International Bible Society, used by permission, Zondervan Bible Publishers; New American Standard Bible (NASB), © 1973 by The Lockman Foundation; New Revised Standard Version Bible (NRSV), © 1989 by the Division of Christian Education of the National Council of the Churches of Christ in the United States of America; the King James Version (KJV), © 1961 The National Publishing Co; the Revised Standard Version (RSV), © 1946, 1952 by the Division of Christian Education of the National Council of the Churches of Christ in the United States of America; the American Standard Edition of the Revised Version (ASV), © 1929 by International Council of Religious Education. Italics in Scripture have been added by the author for emphasis.

"Time In a Bottle" © 1971 Denjac Music Co./MCA Music Publishing (ASCAP). Administered Worldwide by Denjac Music Co. Written by Jim Croce.

"You Don't Mess Around With Jim" © 1971 Denjac Music Co./MCA Music Publishing (ASCAP). Administerd Worldwide by Denjac Music Co. Written by Jim Croce.

DEDICATION

To all of my early church heroes – the L. C. Utleys, the Albert Eslingers, and the Pink Moodys – men whose faith and faces sustained me in times of temptation and who now have gone to their reward.

To my boyhood friends – Sharon Vincent, Doug Bussey, Tommy and Freddy Petersen, and especially to James MacFarland, who always tried to do right.

To my students – who loved me and taught me so much.

To my sister, Jary – what can I say; what words can tell our journey? God bless you, Jary, for all you did, for what you bore, for your understanding and patience.

To my dear niece Priscilla – who meant so much to all of us and has gone to be with Jesus.

To my children – Lincoln, Brendan, Kristen, and Debbie. Thank you for loving me in spite of everything, and thank you for the joy we have gained through the struggles. This book will let you know who your father was, and I pray it will help you know who you are.

To my parents – William Fred and Florence Maria Smith, who loved me enough to teach me about God, His church, and right and wrong; who taught me to love singing, God's Word, and God's people; whose faith formed the foundation of our home and the way we judged value.

To my wife, Judi – who has borne with my moods – the terrible, crushing depressions and skyrocketing exhilarations, who has moved twenty times without complaining or understanding, who has made a home out of almost nothing and with very little help, who has endured more humiliation, deprivation, rejection, and loneliness than any man has a right to expect.

And above all – I dedicate this book to the Creator and Sustainer of the universe, to His only begotten Son, and to that great Spirit who yet moves upon the face of the waters. May this book bring Them praise, glory, honor, and adulation from all who read it.

C O N T E N T S

Contents

♦

viii

Contents

♦

My Mother Played the Piano

My mother played the piano. She played mostly by ear, I think, but she often looked at the notes too. She played "Red River Valley," "When My Blue Moon Turns to Gold Again," and "Mexicali Rose" – but mostly she played church songs. My dad was a member of a church-songbook club, of some sort, and they were always sending us a new songbook. My dad would sit in his chair for hours, singing, "Do-so-mi-do," as he tried to learn all the songs in the new book.

My mother played them on the piano.

It seems, now, that she mostly played in the early- or mid-afternoon. During the summer months, I would approach our little white house, and through the open windows – with the white curtains moving with the breeze – I would hear her playing and singing.

"From this valley they say you are going.
We will miss your bright eyes and sweet smile.
For they say you are taking the sunshine
That has brightened our pathways awhile.

Come and sit by my side, if you love me.
Do not hasten to bid me adieu,
Just remember the Red River Valley
And the girl who has loved you so true."

It was a very comforting, reassuring sound.

Sometimes when I came in to get a drink or some needed thing or to ask if I could go farther than normal, she would say, "John, come here and sing this with me." She didn't say it like a command or an order or anything

– not like when she said, "Go clean the chicken coop," or "Go hoe the garden." Those were orders. She would just say it like a request or like she would appreciate it as a favor.

I usually didn't want to. I was afraid my friends would hear through the open windows – or, worse yet, that they would ask, "What took you so long?" And I would have to say, "I was singing some church songs with my mother," and I could just imagine the looks they would give me – like my driveway didn't go all the way to the street, or something.

I made every possible excuse I could. Of course, I didn't just say "no." You can't do that with requests, you know; and besides, I didn't say that word to my parents. The "N" word was the death word, and if I said it – even in fun – I would die.

I always knew that.

"Come on, John," she would coax. "It will only take a minute."

"Oh Mom," I would say, "Oh, *Mother*" – the exasperation and disgust would absolutely drip from my voice – but I would go, dragging my reluctant feet.

She would be so enthusiastic. She would say, "Now, I want you to sing this alto part for me." I hated that because, even though I was small, I knew that alto

was a woman's part.

"Why do I have to always sing alto? Why can't I sing bass?"

"Because your voice hasn't changed."

"Why does my voice have to change? Did your voice change?"

"No, my voice didn't change, but yours will, and I really don't have time to discuss this. Just sing alto because it sounds nicer with soprano."

"But I want to know why my voice has to change? Did Dad's voice change?"

"Yes, your father's voice changed long before I knew him."

"How do you know his voice changed if you weren't there?"

"Because all men's voices change."

"Did Jary's voice change?"

"No, women's voices don't change."

"But that doesn't seem fair. Why should boys' voices change and not girls'?

"Because that's the way God made us, that's why."

"Oh. Why didn't you just tell me that to begin with?"

And Mom would play the soprano part while she sang it, and then she would play the alto part and sing it. Then she would play the alto part while

I sang it. Then she would play the chords, and I would sing alto while she sang soprano. You can't imagine how excited she would be when we finished. "Isn't that just the prettiest song you ever heard?" she would exclaim. If I thought it was something less than that —

I certainly kept it to myself.

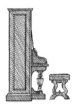

I played my role halfheartedly at best. I had learned that the quickest way back outside was to learn my part as rapidly as possible, but sometimes I just couldn't get into it and sang so poorly and was so sour faced and sullen that she would slowly close the book, pat me on the shoulder, and say, "You go on back to your friends, now. We'll do this some other time." She didn't say it with anger — or even resentment — and I don't know how many times it happened before I noticed that when I went back outside, I didn't hear the piano or singing any more that day.

It wouldn't have cost me much — and it meant so much to her. I look back with regret and tears for my selfishness and insensitivity.

My mother played the piano and sang church songs. Sometimes now — even after all these years — when I can find a place where it is still and if I allow myself to be very quiet, in my mind I can see the old white house with the white curtains moving at the open windows; and through those open windows, I see those nimble fingers moving on the keys, and I hear her voice.

"There's a land that is fairer than day,
And by faith we can see it afar;
For the Father waits over the way,
To prepare us a dwelling place there.
In the sweet by and by,
We shall meet on that beautiful shore.
In the sweet by and by,
We shall meet on that beautiful shore."
—S. F. Bennett, "Sweet By and By"

"Come on, John," she coaxes. "It will only take a minute. You sing alto — it goes like this — and I'll sing soprano. Isn't that the most beautiful song you ever heard?" And in my mind I say, "I'm coming Mom," and I rush to her with joy, because I know how happy it will make her.

And it is, you know,
the most beautiful song
I ever heard.

Introducing the Introduction

I wrote an introduction because every book is supposed to have one, you know. Of course, very few people ever read introductions because they don't read like the rest of the book. So I thought that I ought to introduce my introduction. If you read my introduction – you mustn't be either encouraged or discouraged – because it's not like the rest of the book. It's really a very good introduction – as introductions go. I've read it myself and found it quite interesting and reasonably entertaining.

You might as well go ahead and read it – I mean, you already bought the book – and paid good money for it. It would be a great waste of my time and your money if you didn't.

Introductions tell you in about four or five pages what it takes the rest of the book two hundred pages to say – except that they're sort of dry, stuffy, and text-bookish. This one is a little better. On a scale of one to ten, it rates about a six – in my estimation. If you think it rates lower than that – please don't tell me – a person can only take so much rejection.

If you read the introduction and really enjoy it – we're in deep trouble. If you can still get a refund on the book, you probably ought to. If you don't enjoy it – take heart. I mean, if you say to yourself – "Well, I guess that was okay, but two hundred pages of that would be a little more happiness than I could stand all lumped together in one package" –

then proceed in hope.

Introduction

This is a book about *life*. Actually, it's about my life — which isn't so terribly important except that I'm convinced there is a thread of commonality in the lives of all of us. When you read this book, you're supposed to *remember,* and those memories should bring a smile to your face, a tear to your eye, a reverence to your heart —

and make you better.

If you like good stories, I think you'll like this book. Stories of times gone by instill in us a consciousness of who we are — they give us a sense of *history* — and they help us understand the link that connects the past with the future.

When people see no relationship between themselves and their past, they feel isolated and disconnected. This feeling of disenfranchisement — which is sort of like a broken electrical circuit — destroys any sense of relationship by breaking down our bridges to the past and the future — leaving us isolated.

In order to reestablish our link with the past, we must retrace our steps. There is nothing to sustain us in our present direction — we must *go back*. We must rebuild basic family consciousness. I mean not only the immediate family of parents and children, but the extended family of grandparents, aunts, uncles, and cousins, and ultimately —

the human family.

In a society of fragmented families, far too many children grow to physical maturity with no sense of belonging, no investment in anything larger than themselves. *Storytelling* is a way of teaching and preserving family traditions, which allow children to see themselves as a part of and vital to an ongoing history. It gives them a definite connection to the past and obligates them to the future. Their whole concept of self-worth rests upon this identification.

Most of the stories in this book are from my childhood – some of them are from my children's childhood, some are from other people's experiences. People are always taking me off to the side and asking me if these stories really happened. Now, what kind of question is that? It sure takes the fun out of things. I think what is important is the *truth*. Did the parables Jesus told really happen? I mean, was there really a pearl merchant who sold all of his pearls to buy one big one?

For thousands of years, stories were the measure of truth, and they can still be used effectively in that way. Stories place truth in perspective. They give truth flavor by attaching names, faces, and geographical locations to abstract notions and emotional realities. I believe that all of these stories are true in that sense –

and in that sense, they are all parables.

Introduction

♦

I heard the following story from Fred Craddock, an instructor at the Candler School of Theology at Emory University in Atlanta, Georgia. It was originally told by Scott Momaday, a Kiowa Indian, writer, and literature professor at Southern California University.

Momaday says that when he was a small boy living in a Kiowa Village, his father awakened him unexpectedly very early one morning. He told him to get up and get dressed. He led a very sleepy Momaday by the hand to the house of an old squaw. He left him there and promised to return that evening. This process was repeated over an extended period of time.

All day this ancient squaw told him the stories – sang him the songs of the Kiowa nation. She explained the rituals and the history of the Kiowa – how they began in a hollow log on the Yellowstone River – how they migrated westward. She told of wars with other tribes – of blizzards, cold, and famine. She told him of great chiefs, heroic deeds, and buffalo hunts. She told of the coming of the white man – the clash and the war – of moving north, of moving – always moving – Kansas – Nebraska. She told of diminishing numbers, desperation, and finally – Fort Sill, Oklahoma. She told of the surrender, the reservation, confinement, despair – and the determination to survive.

Finally, the time of his education was over. Momaday says, "I left her house a Kiowa. I knew what it meant to be a Kiowa. I knew who I was and who my people were, and I knew that I would always be a Kiowa."

Look back into your past; remember who you are and who your people were. And then tell those stories to your children. If you can't think of any, read the ones in this book; and in them, you will find your own story. You can simply use them as a point of departure –

"That story reminds me of the time . . ."

It is my prayer that quite often, as you read this book, you will find yourself putting it down with a sigh and saying to yourself – "Yes, that is exactly the way it is." And it doesn't matter if the action was right or wrong – because if it was right, you need to imitate it, and if it was wrong, you need to avoid it.

My ultimate goal is that you look to the Giver and Creator of life – incorporating His wisdom and nature into your own – and become more and more like Him.

Is it really that simple?

My goodness, no. Don't you understand how difficult it is to become like God?

Simple? I guess not!

Introduction

♦

ONE

Mothers

To a very large extent, I am what I am because of my mother. Even more than my father's, my mother's faith, character, and personality are reflected in my life.

Mothers

Mothers are special. Two things about my mother made lasting impressions on me. The first was her "thereness" – by which I mean that she simply was always there. She was there for breakfast, lunch, supper, weekends, after school, and special occasions. She was there when I went to bed, when I got dressed for school, when I was sick in the middle of the night, and when I came home late. During the good times and the bad – *mother* was there. Dad spent long hours at work or with his friends or off on errands – mother was there. She always had time for me, and she was always interested in what I was doing.

The second impression, I will simply call her "faith." It was the most dominant, tenacious, unyielding, pervasive aspect of her being. When I was small, I simply accepted it. Now that I have had to wrestle with doubts and fears to maintain my own faith – I marvel at hers. She read her Bible every day. I mean *every* day – not just for five minutes, but for extended periods. And she didn't just read – she studied, memorized, and meditated – and she *believed*. Yes, my mother believed what she read, and that faith formed the foundation of her life, her love, her conversation, her relationships, and her notions of right and wrong.

Her faith permeated our home.

My mother had many faults. As a child, of course, I did not see her idiosyncrasies as faults – I didn't even see them as idiosyncrasies. As I grew older, her faults became more obvious to me. She had a terrible, unreasonable fear of poverty, which drove her to exhaustion trying to prevent it. It also caused her to be frugal – miserly is a better term – to a degree that painfully affected the whole family. She was extremely opinionated and expressed her opinions with great vigor, often at the expense of other people's feelings. She had a difficult time being happy – it was almost as if she thought it was ungodly.

I reached a point in my early adulthood where my mother's faults began to dominate my feelings toward her, and I must admit that I was impatient – and even disagreed sharply with her. By God's grace, many of my memories of what she had told me about her childhood eventually returned to me, and I marveled at how far she had come and at how much better a home she had given me than what she had had.

Today, I honor her memory. To a very large extent, I am what I am because of her. Even more than my father's, my mother's faith, character, and personality are reflected in my life.

When children grow up – especially sons – they think that their mothers are foolish, sentimental, overprotective, and old-fashioned. They find themselves saying things like, "Oh, Mother, for heaven's sake, I'm twenty years old," or "Yes, of course I'll be careful." Fortunately, they soon become husbands and fathers –

and somehow that cures them pretty quickly.

Mothers

♦

Learning to Read

My mother taught me to read. She didn't mean to – I mean, she wasn't trying to – but she did. I don't know when she began the practice, but I do know that from my earliest remembrances, she read to me every day before I took my nap – except Saturday and Sunday. On weekdays, my father would be at work and my sister at school, so we would crawl into my parents' bed and prop the pillows up against the iron posts of the bedstead – after fluffing them, of course. What a shame that modern children don't even know the word *fluffing*. They don't know it because they don't *fluff* – you can't with polyester and foam rubber. We've added *microchip* to our vocabulary and deleted *fluffing*. It was a sorry exchange, and our language is the more barren for it. Anyway, we would fluff the pillows, nestle back into them, huddle very close to each other, and she would read.

What did she read? The Bible of course – what else? It was the only book in our house. She read stories from the Bible.

She was a finger reader.

Mothers

8

Years later, when I went to school, I read the same way; but my teacher, Miss Smokey, absolutely forbade it. I told her my mother read that way, and she said it was okay for my mother, but not for me. Miss Smokey was very nice – and she meant well – but I'm really glad that my mother's teacher didn't forbid her to read with her finger, because, if she had, you see, I wouldn't have learned nearly so soon or so well, and I might not have loved it so.

Oh, you may not know what finger reading is. It's like fluffing, I guess. Finger reading is following the words with your finger so you won't lose your place or jump to the wrong line. It makes perfectly good sense if you think about it. In schools, nowadays, we're very concerned with how *fast* people read – if you can read a thousand words a minute, that is absolutely fantastic – and it really doesn't matter if you *understand* the words or *enjoy* them or take the time to *think* about them. You must learn to read them very quickly – because there are so many of them – and if you don't read quickly – my goodness – you may never read all of them. And reading all of them is terribly important, even though many of them –

aren't worth much.

My mother was a finger reader. Every day as she read, I would hear her voice and watch her finger as it went back and forth across the page. Of course it happened very slowly – and I didn't *know* I was learning to read. I honestly didn't mean to learn – it was quite an *accident*. Gradually, I began to associate what my mother was saying with the word above her finger. I guess I learned the *and*s, *that*s, and *but*s first – because there are so many of them – but it was easy for an uncluttered mind to grasp that it took a long time to say *Belshazzar* and that it also took a lot of letters; so I began to learn big words too. The more I learned, the more fascinated I became with my mother's voice and her moving finger.

One day I corrected her. She either mispronounced or skipped a word – I don't remember which – and I corrected her. She was incredulous. "How did you know that?" she asked. I didn't know how I knew; I just knew that the word she said wasn't the word that was above her finger. I didn't know the alphabet – that would come much later in school. I didn't know phonics – I still don't. But anybody who can tell the difference between a telephone pole and a fire hydrant can tell the difference between Jehu and Jerusalem. My mother asked me to read, and I did it gladly – slowly, haltingly – finger under the words. With her coaching, I read. Then I read with no coaching, and we took turns. Mom read one day – I read the next.

When I went to school a couple of years later, Miss Smokey tried to teach me to read. I told her I could already read. I could tell it hurt her feelings, so I said I was sorry – but reading was a piece of cake. They were reading Dick and Jane, and I knew Nebuchadnezzar, Jebusite, Perizzite, Shamgar, and Rehoboam. I told her she could teach me math –

I was real dumb in that.

But I want you to see – that if my mother was teaching me to read – without meaning to – she was also teaching me about God, about right and wrong, about good and evil. Yes, those ideas were forming in my mind – waiting for the moment when I would need them to help me understand my growing, changing world.

She didn't mean to – any more than she meant to teach me to read. She read the Bible because she loved to read the Bible – because it had great meaning to her. If I hadn't been around, she would have read it anyway; and after I went to school and didn't take naps anymore, she continued to read. She only knew that it entertained me and that it was good for me in some general way.

My specific point is that both teaching me to read and teaching me about God – about good and evil and standing for the right – did not come to me through lectures and sermons – although I heard plenty of them at church – they came to me through my mother's attempt to establish and strengthen her own relationship with God.

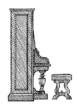

Her daily awareness of His providence,
her constant devotion to Him
and to His Word passed to me –
naturally.

Mother's Cherry Tree

My mother loved all growing things. We had apple trees, pear trees, a grape arbor, a rose arbor, tulips, lilacs, irises, and an annual garden. The Murdocks, who lived directly west of us, had a large cherry orchard. Although they gave us all the cherries we wanted, my mother was determined to have her own cherry tree. Accordingly, one fall we planted (I say "we," because I dug the hole) a three-foot sapling. Mother fertilized, watered, watched over, pampered, and stroked that tree until it was a wonder it didn't die from too much attention. It was amazing how it grew, and in its second spring, it actually blossomed and bore cherries – not enough to make a pie – but my mother was so proud of the accomplishment that she nearly burst. She even carried some of those cherries in her purse to show her friends.

We always shopped at the A & P grocery store in Royal Oak. Fortunately for me, just down the street was Frentz & Sons Hardware. While my mother shopped, I wandered up and down the aisles of Frentz & Sons. It was a fascinating place. Great bins of nails, rows of hinges, racks of shovels, balls of twine – smells of feed, seed, leather goods – and a hundred other items all combined to make it a whole world in itself.

Inevitably, I was led to the fishing equipment, then the gun rack, and finally to the knife display case – which was a wooden cabinet with a glass door. I stood for long minutes gazing in wonder that there were so many fine things to be had. At the bottom of the knife case there was one item in particular that attracted me. It was a belt hatchet –

just the right size for me.

It had a leather case that could be strapped right onto your belt for carrying purposes. I began to pester my mother about it. One day she actually went in to look at it, and I knew that my pleading was getting somewhere. It was a long process, but eventually she bought it for me.

I remember going around the yard whacking on things. It was exceedingly sharp. I whacked on old two-by-fours; I whacked apart an old crate that had been sitting behind the chicken coop – but it was all very dissatisfying. I wanted something more substantial to cut. All of the trees on our place were far too large for me to tackle with my hatchet – all except one – the cherry tree. As preposterous as this seems, the idea was probably enhanced by my school teacher telling us about George Washington cutting down the cherry tree. Since George was quite a hero, the idea of cutting down our cherry tree was an easy step.

I guess that just walking up and cutting it down all at once was a little too much for me; so I decided to *trim* it a little first. The result was that I left not a single limb intact. Our cherry tree was reduced to a forlorn-looking, tapering rod protruding from the ground. Around its base lay a pile of limbs with the leaves looking limp and sickly.

When I stepped back to survey my work, my conscience began. You know, consciences are often the most useless things. When I needed it was before I started, but it was completely silent then – didn't help me a lick. It never said, "John, you'd best think about this," or "Are you sure this is what you want to do?" *Now,* when it was too late to be of any use whatsoever, here it came – full blast. "Now look what you've done," it cried. Pictures of my mother fertilizing and watering, her proud tones as she displayed those first cherries to all of her friends – all flooded my memory and made me feel terrible.

But what good did it do to feel terrible
after the fact?

It also occurred to me that this might not be easy to explain. I put my hatchet in its case and wandered slowly into the kitchen. I had studied some on how best to approach this situation and had decided that it would be to my best advantage to open the subject before it was discovered.

"I know a little boy who cut down a cherry tree," I piped in my most cheerful, winning voice.

My mother, busily occupied, laughed and replied, "Oh, I bet I know who it was. It was George Washington." She said it so nice and sweet that I was reassured and plunged ahead.

"No, it wasn't. It was John Smith."

Right off, there was a noticeable change in both the temperature and the atmospheric pressure in the kitchen. My mother turned on me quickly, and her voice didn't have any sweetness in it – or light either, for that matter.

"Did you cut down my cherry tree?" She grabbed me by my left ear (she was right handed; so her grip was better), and we marched out to the scene of the crime – with her nearly lifting me off the ground, using my left ear for leverage.

I would have gone anyway.

When she saw the tree, she started to cry; and since she needed both hands to dry her eyes, she turned loose of my ear – which was a great relief. It was a sad looking sight, standing there like a little flagpole – but I thought things might go a little easier for me since she was so sad and all. They didn't. She whipped me with every last limb I had chopped off that tree – whipped me till the limb was just shreds of bark left in her hand. I was afraid she was going to start on pear tree limbs, but she finally gave out. You know, a person is mortally strong when they're aroused like that, and they also have an amazing endurance. It cheered me some to think that she was using the *limbs* on me –

instead of the hatchet.

You know, my mother went right back to work on that cherry tree. She kept right on watering and fertilizing and caring for it. Anyone else would have given up. She willed that tree to live, and it did. It grew and became a fine tree, with only a few scars on its trunk – to remind me of my folly.

Children are more like cherry trees than you might think. If they get the right attention, it's amazing how they'll grow. Parents, it's your job to water and fertilize – and yes, you have to do some "trimming" every now and then, too. That's what my mother and dad did for me. The watering and fertilizing part is easier, because kids like that, but the trimming was always painful – for both of us.

Mothers

Today, I am healthy and strong, with only a few scars to remind me of my folly and the trimming my parents did, and I stand here knowing Christ because both He and my mother

wouldn't quit on me.

♦

12

Two Notes

Following are two notes. They reveal much about my mother – and about me. They are printed here exactly as I wrote them. They were written about thirty years apart. The first one I wrote when I was seven or eight. I have no specific memory of the occasion, but when my mother died, I found this note among her treasures. She had saved it for thirty years – through a multitude of moves – through good times and bad –

she hung on to this note.

Dear Mother
I have come
home from camping
had a lot of fun.
I came home for a while
I got here abut
20 to one I have
gone ice shaving
at the pond I
will make sure
I will not get
hurt at all

John
Will be home in
hour or two

Mothers

♦

13

Written in the winter, either 1943 or 1944.

January 24, 1975
8:15 a.m.

Dear Mother,

I am on an airplane to Michigan to see you. Jary called last night to say that you had a severe stroke and that you hadn't regained consciousness.

This sickness and the thought of your impending death has given me cause to consider some things. I feel a very deep need to ask your forgiveness for my extreme selfishness in failing time and again to show proper and Christian consideration to you and your needs. I have failed to do a multitude of small things that I thought of and knew they would please you — yet just didn't do them. I feel that you have endured more from me than anybody has a right to expect, even from a mother.

It is my prayer that if we have a future here that I will, with God's grace be a better son, and a better christian than I have been. God has brought me very low. I praise His Name for what He has shown me about myself.

John

Mom never read the second note — at least not with her physical eyes. She died without ever regaining consciousness. The notes say much — they contain great truths. I never got to be a better son. Hopefully, I have become a better man. And that, of course, is what she wanted me to be — a better man. It is my prayer that you sons and daughters who read this will weep for your failures to be the sons, daughters, husbands, wives, fathers, and mothers that you could have been. It is my prayer that you will (by God's grace) be motivated to become what you ought to be.

Mother's Day

In 1944 our country was engaged in a world war. I was seven. A member of our family had been killed at Pearl Harbor, so the war was very real to us. My mother read daily newspaper accounts of death tolls and of battles won and lost. It was a frightening time.

My father worked long hours at a converted Chrysler automobile factory – now simply called *The Tank Arsenal*. He did not get home till very late at night. Because we lived in a rural setting, my mother was often very apprehensive during his absence and refused to go to bed until he got home. We passed the time waiting for his arrival by singing. My mother would play the piano, and she and my sister and I would sing. We sang, "Red River Valley," "You Are My Sunshine," and "I've Been Working on the Railroad." We sang church songs too – "Sweet Hour of Prayer" and "When We All Get to Heaven." My father was from Arkansas, and he had taught us some Deep South songs like, "Old Kentucky Home," "The Camptown Races," and "Old Black Joe."

One night, after singing long, I went to bed before my father came home. The song "Old Black Joe" remained on my mind.

"Gone are the days,
When my heart was young and gay.
Gone are my friends,
From the cotton field away.
Gone from the earth
To a better land I know.
I hear their gentle voices calling,
'Old Black Joe.'
'I'm commin', I'm commin',
For my head is bending low,'
I hear their gentle voices calling,
'Old Black Joe.'"

I don't know why that song made such a profound impression on me – maybe it was the war and thoughts of death – or maybe it was the uncertainty we all felt – but my child's heart was moved. I felt so sad for Old Black Joe that I began to cry, and the more I cried, the harder I cried. My mother heard me crying and came to my room. She sat on my bed in the dark and stroked my head and held me. She asked me what was wrong, and I told her I didn't like that song about Old Black Joe because it made me think about dead people and sad things, and I thought he must have been terribly mistreated to be so sad.

My mother told me that there was much grief in the world – and much injustice. She said that dying wasn't always such a bad thing – that sometimes it was better than living. She said that Old Black Joe wanted to be with his friends and that now he was – that heaven was a nice place and that God had a very special place for Old Black Joe and his friends and that they were having a good time together.

I went to sleep so happy for Old Black Joe and loving God, who was so nice to him. I was glad that Old Black Joe was having a good life there, because he had had such a bad one here.

I really believed what my mother told me,
and I still believe it to this very day.
I trusted her completely.

Sometimes – Mother's Day, especially – I miss her till I ache. I miss her steadfast faith in a loving God, and I wish I could lay my head in her lap and she would stroke my head and soothe my fears. I believe that God has a special place for my mother, and that she and her friends are happy and singing with Old Black Joe and his friends.

My mother shared her faith with me.
Her faith was the foundation of my faith.

"For I am mindful of the sincere
faith within you, which first dwelt in
your grandmother Lois, and your
mother Eunice, and I am sure that it
is in you as well."
—2 Timothy 1:5 NASB

Mothers

♦

16

Pancho

I've heard it said that dogs take on the personalities of their owners, and if that's so, old Pancho's previous owner must have been the most miserable grunt of all time. I can't remember where my mother got him, but he had short, black, curly hair, and he was totally irascible – Pancho never had a good day in his life. He didn't like any of us – except my mother, and I never thought he really liked her. It was an act he put on so he could keep the perfect situation he had fallen into. He was mean tempered. Every time I approached him, he pulled his lips back and snarled deep in his throat.

Nobody ever petted him or spoke to him – except Mom. She bought him the best food, curried and brushed his coat, fussed and made over him till the rest of us were sick. She said we were just jealous because he wouldn't take up with us – and maybe we were. I always hoped he'd run off, but he was too smart for that. He knew he'd never get another ticket like the one he had; so he rode it and milked it for all it was worth –

and in a dog's world, it was worth plenty.

Now that you know how I felt about Pancho, you won't be surprised at my reaction when I saw him sort of limping around behind the house and acting like he was sick. "What's the matter, you vicious old bugger? Did you try to bite some little girl and get the slats kicked out of you?" I said. He didn't pay any attention – but then he never did – so I went inside. I told my mother that Pancho was acting funny, and she became very concerned.

"What do you mean, 'funny'?" she asked.

"I mean he didn't snarl or try to bite me when I walked by, and he was limping."

Mom ran outside to check on him, but she was back in a moment. She said he wouldn't come out of his doghouse and wanted me to go and check on him. I tried to coax him out, but he wouldn't come, so I reached in – and true to form, he tried to bite me. I jerked my hand back and told my mother that I hoped he had leprosy, the jungle rot, and Asiatic flu. I said I hoped his temperature would go to about two hundred degrees and damage his brain so he would be more normal. I was real upset. She tried to get me to make another attempt, but I told her just to let him sleep it off.

When I went back that evening after supper, he was dead – "deader than a doorknob," as we used to say. I don't know why we selected doorknobs, almost anything else would have done just as well – but it's pretty graphic when you think about it. It would be nice to say that I was sorry and that

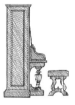

I regretted doing mean things to him – but it wouldn't be true, because I wasn't. But mother was. She cried and carried on, and we all felt bad for her because she really loved Pancho –

in spite of all his faults.

I dug the hole, and we buried Pancho out behind the house under the apple tree. It was just the three of us – Mom, Dad, and I – and we didn't say anything – but she wanted us there for the burial. I looked out the window late that evening and saw my mother standing beside the grave grieving. For as long as we lived there, when evening came and I couldn't find my mom, I knew where she would be. When we moved from that house, when the last of the furniture was loaded and we were ready to go, we couldn't find her, and Dad said, "I know where she is" – and so did I. I can see her there yet.

She kept a picture of Pancho playing ball with her on her dresser, and for years she talked lovingly of her favorite pet.

Pancho died without a friend in the world except my mom. But that was like her. She was always picking up strays, sticking up for folks that no one else had anything good to say about. She was always ready to help people who would never be able to return the favor, and even when they returned her help with meanness or betrayal, she'd go right back and help again if they needed her.

I learned a lot from my mom.

Mothers

♦

18

Where Did It Go?

She really didn't want to go, but she had taken the boy to the holiday pageant because she wanted to be a good mother. It was about what she'd expected – poorly done, old costumes, missed lines, a hackneyed, trite repeat of familiar words and tunes, with the characters played by less than amateurs.

The boy had been fascinated by *the star*. It was the only really well-done piece in the set. Someone had obviously put some time, experience, and thought into it. It revolved, high above the stage, sparkling and twinkling, constantly bringing back even an unwilling gaze. The boy had asked what it was, and she had given the old stock answer.

She was relieved when it was finally over.

It was dark when they left, very dark, and very cold, but it was marvelously clear. She hurried toward the car and regretted that she had had to park so far away. She kept his hand in hers, and when he stumbled, she almost fell with him.

"Watch where you're going," she said – perhaps more crossly than she intended. She stopped to help him to his feet.

"I was looking for the star," he said apologetically.

"Why, there's millions of them," she misunderstood.

"I was looking for *His* star," he corrected.

"Oh, don't be silly, honey. That was just a play – people acting. The star went away long ago. You can't see it anymore."

"Where did it go? How do you know you can't see it anymore?" He was disappointed but continued to look.

"I don't know where it went, honey; it just went away, and that's why you can't see it. Come on now; we've got to hurry."

"Maybe it's that one!" He pointed to a particularly bright, friendly star. "Is that Jesus' star?"

"No, honey, it's not Jesus' star. It's just a bright star."

"But it *could* be His star," he insisted. "Maybe it's come back."

Across her consciousness there flashed *a thought*. Where it came from, who could guess? Some might say that the Spirit, ever watchful, never sleeping, seized this precious moment when her guard was down and kindled into flame a thought, a thought that had lain dormant for years.

"Oh God," she thought, "I wish it were His star; I wish it had come back –

I wish I could believe in it like I used to."

She did not say it out loud, but it was there – and then it was blotted out by cold, fatigue, and pressing cares – but not completely. It was a prayer, and it was heard in the heart of Him who hears the beating of our hearts and knows our every thought – and who waits for moments like these to work His will in our lives. Before she had thought of what to say to her son, His messengers were speeding faster than light to respond.

Mothers

♦

19

At the boy's insistence, she finally looked up, and there was a star! I mean, it was as different from other stars as a bonfire is from a kitchen match. She glanced quickly down at her small son, and the soft, iridescent glow of the star seemed to cast a gentle halo of light all around him. And then it was gone, and she shook her head like one who wishes to make certain of her alertness.

When they got home, she was still troubled by it. She helped the boy undress, and she tucked him in with more care and tenderness than usual. When he asked her to help him with his prayers, she did – and she added a special, new prayer of her own. "Dear Father," she said, "I'm not sure just what happened tonight, but thank you."

When she returned to the living room, her husband, without looking up from the TV, said, "Well, how did it go?"

"If you really cared how it went, you might try going sometime. It went about the same as last year when you didn't go with us – except . . . " and her voice trailed off into silence, and she couldn't find a way of finishing.

He looked up from the show he was watching. "Except what? Did something happen?"

"No, nothing you would be interested in."

"Hey, I'm sorry I didn't go.

Did I miss something?"

"Yes, as a matter of fact, you *did* miss something. You missed being with your son and making him think he is more important than that stupid show. You missed being with me and letting me know that I am more important than that stupid show. You miss a lot of things, Andy, but tonight you missed something – something *really* special."

She paused, her heart beating wildly because she knew she was making a leap into the darkness – but she knew she had to take the chance. She picked up the remote control and flipped the TV off.

"You're really cranked up about this, aren't you? Did something happen?"

"Yes," she said. "Yes, something *did* happen, Andy – at least I think it did, although I'm not sure just what – but it's not what happened that really matters. What matters is that it made me start thinking, and we need to talk."

And they did, you know.
They talked and talked.
And things were never the same again.

At some point in every holiday season, I find myself gazing at the stars. They seem especially close and significant when it's cold and silent. I think

I want to see *that* star, at least to imagine the *wonder* of it, as it makes its majestic and purposeful way to its appointed destination. There, where it concentrates its glorious radiance on the holy ground, is where Jesus was born. God, calling to us —

"Look over here.
See my Incarnation."

It's not too hard for me to believe in *that* star. My child's heart, awakened from months of slumber by this blessed season, is fully confident that its guiding light brought those wise men to worship Jesus. I wonder, though — where did it go? Does God still move stars to serve His purpose? Is there yet a light calling us to Bethlehem? Does His star not shine for us because we have grown so mature and practical that we dismiss it, as Scrooge dismissed his ghosts by uttering a *"Humbug!"* of disbelief?

The star was for *all* to see, but only the wise men were guided by it. When they arrived, they did not find multitudes of seekers who had also followed its light. Perhaps the guiding light of God's special star is there yet, but our eyes are not pointed upward to Him — because we do not believe in stars. Our eyes look inward to our own wisdom and outward to our own light and around us to the light and wisdom of people like ourselves. And all the while, God calls us by His light, pleading with us to look upward to His holiness.

A child's imagination is a marvelous gift of God. Encourage it; strengthen it. The world will be struck real all too soon — you needn't worry about that. Sometimes we would all do well to see God through the eyes of a child. All together too many imaginations are ridiculed and discouraged by grownups who no longer have the capacity to dream.

Where did it go?

Mothers

◆

21

Oh, Really

We moved from Allen Park, Michigan, back to Royal Oak when I was a sophomore in high school. I didn't know too many people there, but I struck up a tentative friendship with a boy who sang first tenor next to me in the a cappella choir. One day we were talking before practice began – that inquisitive, casual but probing kind of talk that ultimately determines whether your friendship rises or falls. He told me where his father worked and what an important position he held. I told him that my dad sold batteries and electrical parts for cars.

He asked if I was familiar with a certain ladies' fashion store in town. When I said I had heard of it, he said – with an air of unconcealed pride – that his mother owned that store and was responsible for its operation. Not to be outdone, I quickly related that my mother worked for Judge Arthur E. Moore. When he asked what she did, I said she was a housekeeper. He was obviously impressed by the name, but he was uncertain about the term "housekeeper." When he inquired as to what a housekeeper did, I said that she cooked, cleaned, made beds, and did laundry for them.

"You mean your mother is a *cleaning lady?*" His tone was slightly incredulous.

I said that I guessed that was right, but I had never thought about it exactly in those terms.

He turned to the boy sitting beside him and said, "Hey, John's mother is a *cleaning lady.*"

"Oh, really," the boy responded. There was no mistaking the tone.

> For the first time in my life,
> I wished my mother had a different job.

It bothered me all day. It occurred to me on my way home that I had never thought of my mother as a *cleaning lady*. I thought of her, more than anything, as my mother. I thought of her work as being very necessary and useful – much more useful than a fashion shop – when it came down to it. I decided that a person needed to know much more about my mother and her work before they were qualified to say,

> "Oh, really."

It was obvious to me, even then, that my friendship with those boys was going to be very limited because of my parents' occupations. I am very sorry to say that I felt the loss deeply. I had no way of knowing then that their friendship was worth about what a ladies' fashion shop is worth – almost nothing. I was ashamed of my mother's job and never, ever mentioned it again to anyone, but it didn't help. There were too many other unmistakable signs about me – signs I didn't even know about and couldn't possibly cover up. I was classified. Son of a Cleaning Lady was the sign I wore. And instead of accepting it with dignity, I languished under its reproach.

It hurts me now to think that I was ever ashamed of my mother or anything about her. I know that children often – especially from junior high through college – are ashamed or embarrassed by some things about their parents. If they have unimportant jobs, if they wear outdated, *nerdy* clothes, if they are much overweight, if they have *old-fashioned* ideas about music or morals or movies, if they drive the wrong cars or are just *out of touch* – kids have a tendency to avoid bringing friends home and often don't want their parents to attend school functions.

Children must be taught to look deeper – to see beyond those transitory, surface evaluations of worth. Parents must not demean other people in their children's presence on such a shallow basis. When your children hear you speak of others, do you sometimes say,

"Oh, really"?

Mothers

♦

23

TWO

Fathers

Sometimes you have to be there for a thousand insignificant moments that are forgotten, in order to be there for that one big moment that is remembered.

Fathers

I firmly believe that our earliest, and often most critical and lasting, notions about God, our heavenly Father, are formed by our earliest notions about our earthly fathers. The way we regard our earthly fathers dictates the respect, the obedience, the honor, and the love with which we regard their presence and directives – and so it is with our heavenly Father. Those notions begin very early and take shape slowly, expanding and being redefined with specific incidents, maturity, and perspective. I think of my father much differently now than I did when he died in 1963.

Mothers are most appreciated when you're small and when you're growing up. Often, fathers don't get appreciated until much later. Sometimes you have to be fifty or sixty before you really understand what they did for you. Fathering never stops – and some of the most important fathering my dad ever did was

when I was grown.

The challenge to today's fathers is to be worthy of the name. Our culture has eroded and demeaned both traditional and biblical concepts, leaving only frustration and confusion. Fathers who are half apologetic for bringing their children into the world; who are so concerned with their children's self-image that they teach them nothing; so afraid of being thought a tyrant – or even worse, out of touch – that they fail to discipline them; who want to be a buddy more than they want to be a father; who bow to their children's every whim, rather than risk offending them; who leave parenting to their wives – these kinds of fathers are very misleading examples of divine fatherhood.

What is a father? Fathers have jobs – they bring home money. Fathers work – even when they're sick, when they hate their jobs, and when they see no hope.

Fathers are fixers. They can fix anything – plumbing, bicycles, lawnmowers, and toy trucks. And when they can't fix it – they say that they don't have the right tools or that we needed a new one anyway or that they don't make them like they used to. They even fix cuts, bruises, and disappointments –

or make them unimportant.

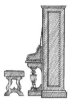

Fathers

Fathers are not afraid of the dark, the neighbor's dog, or the boogie man.

Fathers *should* be storytellers. Almost everything that happens should remind them of another time, and when they tell those stories, they must stop being businessmen, plumbers, electricians, computer programmers, and salesmen – and become the boys they once were – and never will be again –

but they should never stop longing
or trying.

Fathers need to be decision makers. They need to know where they're going, and they need to accept responsibility when they go wrong. Fathers need to defy a culture that seeks to emasculate and feminize them and turn them into junior partners on the family board of directors.

Fathers need to provide spiritual leadership for their families. They should not be ashamed to be seen praying or reading their Bibles. They must be careful to act and talk in harmony with scriptural injunctions and precedents – and when they go wrong – they admit their error, ask forgiveness, pray about it, and leave it behind them.

The Bible portrays four major characteristics of God that every father should emulate. First, God is dependable and consistent. God keeps his word – either *yes* or *no* or *not now*. Second, God is understanding. When we tell God, "It wasn't my fault," he may say, "Yes, it was" or "I know it wasn't" or "It really doesn't matter, now does it?" Third, God is forgiving, which means that sometimes I don't get what I deserve and sometimes I do. Fourth, God is loving, and that means that he always acts in my best interest.

What kind of father are you?
What notions about God do your children have?

And to My Children I Bequeath

My father, William Fred Smith, was born on June 19, 1897. He was born in the city of Poughkeepsie, in Strawberry township, in Sharp County, in the state of Arkansas. His mother, Suzanne Clementine Smith, was 29 when he was born, and he was her seventh child.

He was born at home.

He told me that he finished the tenth grade in school – which, he said, was the last grade there was – and he never had any further education. He had great admiration for his teacher – Cecil Pickens – whom he mentioned often.

He was inducted into the U.S. Army on October 31, 1918, but the war was soon over, so he was discharged on December 24, 1918. He was in the 43rd Company, 11th Battalion, 162nd Depot Brigade. He was one of the nameless, faceless, lack-luster privates who never went anywhere or did anything and who consequently never had any war stories to tell.

He married my mother on October 4, 1930, in Detroit, Michigan. He was thirty-three. On their marriage license he listed his employment as Gas Station Operator.

My sister, Lillian Clementine, was born April 26, 1931, and I was born on March 31, 1937.

William Fred Smith died in Veteran's Hospital in Indianapolis, Indiana, at 3:30 P.M. on October 10, 1963.

My father was the most ordinary, unexceptional, unsuccessful man you can imagine. He was always in debt, he consistently made bad business decisions, he kept our family in constant turmoil with ill-conceived moves, and he quit good jobs and took bad ones. The houses we lived in were often humiliating.

Fathers

♦

32

My mom and dad had marital problems – sometimes serious ones. When you move from town to town with financial ruin facing you and the future holding no hope but a cycle of repetition, there is bound to be trouble. My mom left home two or three times – I think from sheer desperation, trying to find relief from the hopeless cycle of poverty and drudgery that surrounded her. I never knew where she went. My dad would say – "Mom will be gone for a few days." Then she would call, and my dad would go and get her and bring her back.

My dad never left home.

My dad loved to fish – even though he never had the time or the money or the equipment – and he didn't really know much about it. When we went, it was to Bogie Lake – out near Commerce, Michigan. We rented an old wooden boat from Old Man Bogie, and we rowed all over the lake. Sometimes we caught some bluegills, sunfish, and bullheads. We kept everything we caught, and we ate them. The few times we went I remember – I remember nearly everything about them. About the time we got to where we might have gone more – he died.

There were only two or three things that were constant in my life. We always prayed before meals – no matter where we lived or how little we had. We always went to church. Church was the glue that held our family together. It wasn't just services, it was singings, potlucks, work days, Bible studies, gospel meetings, weddings, and funerals. And my dad never grumbled about going – he was always happy – expectant.

The third thing that was constant was that my dad worked every day. It was absolutely heroic. Under the most hopeless circumstances, he never quit. He got up and went to work every day. He had two marvelous gifts – a great singing voice and a great gift for hope. He always believed that something good was going to happen to him. He went to the mailbox every day – expecting it. He didn't know exactly what it was, but he always believed it would come. It never did – but that isn't important,

because his hope kept him going.

I said it never came − actually, that isn't true. On October 10, 1963, at Veteran's Hospital in Indianapolis, Indiana, at about 3:30 P.M., my dad went to the mailbox for the last time − and when he opened it − it was there. The thing he had been looking for and hoping for and expecting all his life. I wish I could have seen his face when he opened it.

What I'm trying to say − what I want you to see − is that my father failed in just about everything − in the army, in education, in sports, at work, in financial matters − in just about everything.

Yes, Dad failed in everything − with one exception. He succeeded in the only thing that matters. I am what I am today, not because of his failures, but because of his only success. If he had succeeded in every other area and failed in this one, he would have truly been a failure.

When my dad died, he left us nothing − unless of course you think that singing − and going to church − and praying before meals − and living in hope − are really worth something.

What do you plan to leave your children?

⚜

Jump

One day, I was playing in our backyard with a paint can lid. It was before the days of Frisbees − perhaps the inventor of the Frisbee got his idea from watching the creative genius of a child who, like me, had discovered the amazing flying propensities of a paint can lid. I was sailing it into the wind, and as its momentum slowed, the wind would take it higher and higher. Then it would begin its downward and backward glide, and I would try to catch it. Eventually, it landed and lodged on the roof of the chicken coop. Since we had no ladder, I got one of our long cane poles that we used for fishing and fretted and worried most of the afternoon trying to dislodge it. I finally gave up.

When my father came home, I met him in the driveway. Before he was out of the car, I began pleading with him to help me to retrieve my toy. He put his lunch pail down on the front porch, and we walked around the house together. He assured me that it was no problem and that we could get it back.

He hoisted me up on his shoulders, then grabbed my feet and boosted me up onto the roof of the chicken coop. He told me to walk very carefully, because the coop was old and decaying. I retrieved my toy and returned to the edge of the coop. I felt very powerful looking down at my father. He smiled up at me and then held out his arms and said,

"Jump."

Even now – forty-five years later – I close my eyes, and I can see him – as plainly as I can see the lake and the trees from where I sit writing this just now. He was so tall, so strong, so confident – with his big, handsome, grinning face – that it is easier for me to imagine that day than the day he died.

I jumped. With no hesitation, I jumped, and he caught me easily and hugged me and then swung me to the ground. He sent me to fetch his lunch pail, and in a moment we were in the house and the incident was forgotten –

no, it wasn't forgotten, was it?

He would be amazed that I remember it – I'm sure that within a very short time, he forgot it. He wasn't trying consciously to be a good father. He didn't come home that day with a plan to create a lasting memory for his son. It wasn't planned at all.

My point is that most parenting cannot be planned for, except in your own personal walk with God and in prayer. Many great opportunities for lasting impressions are either lost or become negatives because you can't fake what you are when the unexpected comes.

If my father had generally been selfishly unconcerned with his children's cares, there would have been no time or cause for him to turn this unexpected moment into a great triumph – he would have acted according to his nature, told me he was much too tired to fool with me, reprimanded me for my carelessness, and gone into the house, leaving me to my own devices –

and the moment would have been lost.

The opportunities come – providentially, unexpectedly – and most of the time we react according to who we are rather than what we ought to be. We serve our children best by constantly seeking to become more closely molded into the image of our Lord Jesus Christ – not by reading how-to manuals on child rearing. We do not become good parents by trying to practice a parenting philosophy that is contrary to our natures. We become good parents — good neighbors, good husbands, and good friends — by becoming *good* —

by turning our lives toward God.

❧

Love's Old Sweet Song

"Just a song at twilight,
When the lights are low
And the flickering shadows
Softly come and go.

Tho' the heart be weary,
Sad the day and long,
Still to us at twilight
Comes Love's old sweet song."
—G. Clifton Bingham, "Love's Old Sweet Song"

During the year that we lived on Gardenia Street in Royal Oak, I got very sick. I think it was some sort of influenza, but the Smith's didn't doctor much, so we never knew. We accepted our sicknesses as a part of God's divine providence, and we worked our way through them as best we could. We cured everything with chicken noodle soup, dry toast, poached eggs, and hot tea. (I highly recommend this remedy to all parents; it has the advantage of not only working, but being very cheap. Its only disadvantages are that it is old and simple.)

I had been sick for several days, and my vomiting, fever, and inability to eat or drink had made me very weak. My mother had stayed at my bedside or close by the entire time. My dad was working at some kind of tool and die shop, so I only saw him in the evenings. When he came home, he would stick his head in the door to see if I was awake. If I was, he'd grin real big and say, "Hey, Bud, how're you doing? You feel like going fishing?" He said it so cheerfully that it made me feel better.

That was at first.

Toward the end, when I was so sick and weak that I could scarcely speak and they had begun to worry, he'd come in and take my hand or rumple my hair a little, and he'd say, "How you feeling, son? Is there anything I can do for you?" His face would be filled with care, and I was sorry to worry him so.

One night, very late, I awoke slowly from my feverish sleep. The light was on in the hallway, and the door to my room was open just a crack. In the shadowy half-light, I could see someone sitting by my bed. I thought it was my mother. I must have moved a little because I felt someone squeeze my hand. I knew it wasn't my mother. The hand was large, strong, and rough. Without turning my head, I moved my eyes slowly in his direction. My dad was sitting – slumped over in a chair. He still had on his work clothes – a light blue shirt and dark blue pants, with heavy black shoes and white socks. There were stains on the shirt, and it smelled that kind of burnt-oil smell that saturated all his shop uniforms. His head was resting in his free hand, his eyes were closed, and there were tears on his face. When I saw his lips move a little –

I knew immediately that he was praying.

My dad was singing "Love's Old Sweet Song" – not those words and not the music, you understand – but the oldest, sweetest song there is. A song that has been sung since the beginning of time. When my heart is weary – sad the day and long – at twilight I remember those days and love's old sweet song. My dad was singing it at its very best. I was eleven.

It is important to see that things like that paid – more than paid – for all of his failures. Even the best of fathers fail much and often – yes, they do – even the best of them. But when the big moments come – the real crises – they have to be there.

And this is really important: You *can't just show up for the big moments* – because, you see – you never know when they will come; so you have to show up *every day*. Sometimes you have to be there for a thousand insignificant moments that are forgotten, in order to be there for that

one big moment that is remembered.

Nowadays we talk about quality time. I hear people say inane things like, "Well, I don't get to spend a *lot* of time with my kids, but when I *am* with them, I make sure it is quality time." Hogwash! We can rationalize anything. How do we *make sure* that it's *quality time?* What is quality time to a child? Is helping with history quality time? Is sitting up with a sick child quality time? Is saying grace before meals quality time?

You simply do not have the power to create quality time. Those moments are providential. Being there *consistently* is the only guarantee of being there when the big moments come.

One of God's most impressive qualities is that

He is the God
who is *there*.

Edith

My father bought the huge, old, two-story house at 723 Gardenia from a man named A. N. Allen. I know because I've still got an ancient, gold pocket watch of his, and it has his initials stamped on it. We always called him "Old Man Allen." When we bought the house, the old man asked if he could stay a *few days* until he found another place to live, and my dad agreed. He slept on an old sofa that was in the dining room.

I was eleven.

We soon discovered that he was a drunk — a pitiful, sad old man who was so enslaved to alcohol that he had lost his job, his family, his friends, and his respect. The few days he wanted to stay with us turned into a nightmare of weeks. He wandered in at every hour of the night — hopelessly drunk, staggering, falling over furniture, cursing, finally collapsing fully clothed on his urine-soaked couch. He slept fitfully until his craving took him once again in search of the only cure to his misery that he knew. My father couldn't bring himself to turn him out into the street. He tried to reason and pray with him –

but it did no good.

He had been married. His wife's name was Edith. She was dead now. The neighbors told us that during her last years, she had been an invalid, confined to the house and mostly to bed. Their children had married and moved far away, so the old man was solely responsible for her care. She would lay for days with no food, no medical attention, unable to get to the bathroom – until the neighbors heard her cries and came to her assistance.

He would be on a binge.

Fathers

Time after time it happened. I do not doubt that he loved her – or had loved her. I do not doubt that he *wanted* to do better – that he determined often that he *would* do better, but he was so completely in the grip of that demon, which tormented, instructed, and directed his every waking moment, that *he forgot her.* She lay alone, uncared for, and one day – in that very condition – she died. She worked her way to the edge of the bed and fell to the floor. She dragged herself to the door, and she called his name, pleading for him to come.

♦

38

And that is where he found her.

Her death and the manner of it haunted him. Those memories drove their way even into the confused, desolate, surrealistic dreams of his drunken stupors. His tortured, delirious voice would cry out in agony, reverberating through the house. It was never more than one word: "Edith" – he would wail in his despair – "E-dith!" – *"E-dith!"* His voice would rise higher and higher until it shattered, cracked, and broke – subsiding quickly into silence. But Edith was beyond his voice, beyond his ability to forget or neglect, or to help or hurt ever again. I lay in my bed and shuddered with the desolation, wretchedness, and despair that tormented him. I can hear that voice yet.

It will always ring in my ears.

I don't know what happened to him. My father was forced to make him leave, finally, and I guess he crawled off into whatever long-forgotten corner that his kind always crawl to, and he died. And no one cared.

My father told me that Old Man Allen had not always been this way. He talked to me about when he was young and handsome, having fun, surrounded by friends – and about how his drinking must have started. My dad talked to me about how someone who probably meant him no harm encouraged him to drink the first one, and the second. He talked to me about the turns of the road where his path might have taken a new direction and about Satan's unwitting cohorts who urged his feet back into the rut – a rut that grew constantly deeper and whose ultimate destination was predetermined.

How is it possible to be understanding toward the sale of alcohol? How can one tolerate the blatant advertising lies, the deliberate, premeditated deceit of an industry that peddles its wares of destruction and hopelessness in the name of good times, good friends, home, family, community pride, the great outdoors, and eternal happiness – and with the ludicrous admonition to "Drink responsibly; know when to say when."

Both my father and God pointedly used this event to embed the dangers of alcohol in my mind. Old Man Allen made such a vivid impression on me that when I was older – and the opportunity and the temptation came to initiate the drinking habit –

I shrunk from it in horror.

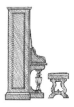

♦

⬯

The Upward Way

The boy was short, and he still had much of what is called *baby fat* in his appearance. He wore glasses, and he was often teased. His school record was far from brilliant, except that he was favored by his teachers because he was well mannered and said "sir" and "ma'am." His father and mother were concerned because he had no victories. He never won at anything. He didn't make any of the teams, he wasn't a brilliant student, he lacked aggressiveness, and he seemed to be constantly withdrawn. He had little enthusiasm for life –

and he was alone much.

Behind the house where they lived were some high mountains topped by great, jagged upthrusts of perpendicular rock. The steep slopes beneath were extremely rugged and forbidding, covered with pin oak brush, cat

claw, cactus, manzanita, ironwood, and ponderosa pine – with an occasional blue spruce. The washes, which carried the spring runoff, cut deep ravines in these slopes and were choked with huge boulders – fallen ages ago – and with log jams of fallen trees, brush, and other debris. The father noticed that the boy looked often toward those craggy summits, gazing long minutes in wonder at their majesty.

One winter day, when the sun was glistening radiantly from the snow-covered peaks, the boy expressed his desire to some day climb to the top. The father determined that his chance would come.

Accordingly, one fine, spring evening – with no warning – the father announced that there would be no school the next day – a special project was planned. The excitement, the anticipation – as they planned what to wear, filled canteens, and packed a lunch – was well worth the effort. They drove their four-wheel drive truck up the mountain as far as the last rut-riddled road would take them, found a promising ravine, and set out.

Those who mounted Everest worked no harder, suffered no greater hardship or discouragement – and had no greater desire to quit. The father had not realized how difficult a task he had set, but he knew they must not fail – the boy *must* accomplish this. Red-faced from exertion, panting hoarsely, and sweating profusely, the boy hinted more than once that perhaps they ought to return.

The heroic ascent continued.

Finally, they broke out into the open, and the panorama of the miles they could see was awesome. Their whole town, tucked away in a fold of lesser hills, looked insignificant. "I'll bet we can see Flagstaff from the top," the boy cried – and they plunged ahead.

When they came to a second opening, they stopped and ate part of their lunch. They rested their weary backs and aching legs against a great ponderosa. They shared a tree, a sandwich, a canteen, a view, a struggle, a hope, their fatigue – and they shared the marvelous silence.

"It sure is quiet, isn't it, Dad?" the boy whispered, as though he were afraid his voice might shatter the calm. "I never heard it so quiet before."

They were close, and it was good.

There was no talk of returning now. When they finally, reluctantly – but with renewed vigor – left their lunch spot, they talked only of how long – how far to the top. They reached it by two o'clock. The last seventy-five yards was hand-over-hand climbing up a nearly vertical, rock-ribbed surface. As they neared the top, their hearts were pounding, and they were absolutely breathless. The father had come behind, to help the boy, to reassure him against falling, and because he wanted him to be first. When the boy finally topped the ascent, he turned – his long, brown hair moving with the wind, some of it stuck to the sweat of his forehead – and stretched out his hands, and said –

"Let me help you up, Dad. It's great."

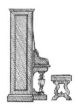

All the Trumpets Sounded

After this it was noised abroad that Mr. Valiant-for-truth was taken with a Summons by the same Post as the other, and had this for a Token that the Summons was true, *That his pitcher was broken at the Fountain.* When he understood it, he called for his Friends, and told them of it. Then said he, I am going to my Fathers, and tho' with great difficulty I am got hither, yet now I do not repent me of all the Trouble I have been at to arrive where I am. My Sword I give to him that shall succeed me in my Pilgrimage, and my Courage and Skill to him that can get it. My Marks and Scars I carry with me, to be a witness for me that I have fought his Battles who now will be my Rewarder. When the day that he must go hence was come, many accompanied him to the River-side, into which as he went he said, *Death, where is thy Sting?* And as he went down deeper he said, *Grave, where is thy Victory?* So he passed over, and all the Trumpets sounded for him on the other side.

—John Bunyan, *Pilgrims Progress*

After dinner, they took the same walk that they always took. The boy knew nearly every step. What he waited for eagerly were the stories his grandfather might tell as things along the way brought back memories. When the boy was small, he had lived quite close to his grandparents, and the Sunday afternoon walks over the farm were regular. Now he lived far away, and he only came during vacations and sometimes on holidays.

Fathers

♦

42

"This is where your grandmother and I built our first house; it burned in 1937. If you look carefully, you can still see the corner of the old foundation.

"See the opening there in the barn right under the eave? That's a hay mow. Your father fell out of there, when he was just about your size, and broke his arm." (The stories were much longer, but we have no patience for long stories.)

"Oh, now, Dad," the boy's father interrupted. "He doesn't want to hear that story again; you've told it ten times."

But the boy's father was wrong, and he wasn't only wrong, he wasn't telling the truth. It was *he* who didn't want to hear the story; it stirred too many painful memories of a happy past – of a life that was so different from his present one – that it didn't seem possible that both lives could have been lived by the same person. The stories reminded him of the contrast between what he had planned and hoped to be – and what he had become –

and the contrast was not something
he was comfortable with.

The boy hadn't realized it – it wasn't part of his consciousness – and he didn't realize it now, but a sense of the significance of family history and his personal identity had come through those walks and stories. Now he was fourteen, and in his jumbled, confused time of physical and mental transformation, the farm and his grandfather were things that gave meaning and perspective to his growing, changing world. Although he would not have said so, he loved his grandfather,

and he loved the stories.

As they approached the windmill, where the steep ascent to the upper pasture began, his grandfather paused – his thin, white hair matted down with perspiration and his normally clear, blue-gray eyes a little misty. "You and your dad go on up," he said to the boy. "These old legs just won't make it up there anymore. I'll just rest here and wait." That had never happened before, and as the boy and his dad walked slowly away, a thought began to gather in the boy's mind. It gained momentum and clarity as he and his father silently climbed to the pasture. Finally, unable to go farther without hearing his thought out loud, he stopped. He looked at his father and said, "Grampa's getting old, isn't he, Dad?"

What a world of budding maturity lay behind those words.

"Yes – Dad, your grandpa, is eighty-five this year." The father was not close to his son because he was very busy, and he had no time to tell him

stories. Because he didn't know his son, he failed to hear what was behind the question.

"Do you think he minds?"

"Yes, I'm sure he does. He can't do much anymore, and he knows that the good part of his life is behind him." He spoke quickly and with some inner bitterness, as though he did not wish to pursue the topic; but the boy could not turn loose of his thought.

"You'll get old, too, won't you, Dad?"

"Yes, you bet I will. I've already started, and I hate it." Again, the bitterness.

"I can't believe I'll ever get old," the boy said.

Fathers

♦

44

"It's hard when you're as young as you are, and all of the good things are in front of you; in fact, I guess that's what being young is all about – all of the important things are in front of you. Why, I remember . . . " he began enthusiastically, but his voice trailed away. The boy had turned in anticipation, anxious to hear his father's story, but his father stopped, shrugged his shoulders in resignation, and said, "Oh, forget it."

"Forget what?"

"Nothing; it was nothing. I thought I remembered something there for a minute, but it's gone."

Two hours later, they returned to the windmill and found the old man asleep, huddled in a corner out of the wind and where the spring sun would fall on him – a shrunken bundle of faded blue denim and wrinkled flesh. His head lay at a precarious angle, and saliva dripped from the corner of his mouth. His breathing was so shallow that the boy feared he had died, but when he touched his shoulder, the kindly, thoughtful, blue eyes blinked in the sun, and he smiled. As they began the walk back, the boy, still pursuing his thought, expressed his concern.

"Dad says you're eighty-five, Grampa. Getting old must be terrible. Dad says that the worst thing is that you don't have anything to look forward to, that all the good and important stuff is behind you."

The old man paused and looked long at his son and then at his grandson.

"I think your father has forgotten that I have been preparing for this all my life," he said solemnly, "that the most important and the very best things are yet to come, and that crossing the great river in front of me is the most important challenge of all."

"River? What river, Grandpa?"

"Ask your father; he knows what river I'm talking about. He needs to remember, and he needs to tell you about it."

Is it time you "remembered" something that your children need to hear?

Who Is Responsible?

When my oldest son, Lincoln, was in the fourth grade, he attended the Maize Unified School District Elementary School, in Maize, Kansas. Maize was a town of about eight hundred souls, I think, although some of them did not know they had souls – or at least they acted as though they did not. But I suspect that it was pretty much like most other towns, in that respect. The town was named after the grain that occupied the labor, time, attention, and conversation of nearly every resident, because their financial well-being and future expectations were tied directly to that product.

It was a good enough school, probably above average as schools go, but at some point I began to be troubled by certain of my son's comments and attitudes. It wasn't anything outlandish, just a series of minor incidents, which taken individually would be passed off as inconsequential, but collectively, spelled trouble. I decided that I would go and visit with his teacher –

which I hoped would put my mind at rest.

I called the school and made an appointment to come the following day, but my apprehension intensified when the teacher returned my call that evening to ask why I was coming. I explained my concern in very non-threatening terms and assured him that I had no reason to doubt either his interest or his competency. He tried to assure me that all was well and that there was no reason for me to come. The more he protested that nothing was wrong, the more determined I was to go. We made an appointment for the next day right after school, and I asked him not to tell my son that I was coming.

I intentionally arrived early and stood just outside the classroom door in the hallway. Through the window in the door, I had a clear view of nearly the whole classroom, and since the students (actually, the word "student" has connotations not appropriate to this group; "occupants" might be a better term) were seated with their backs to the door, I could watch and listen unobserved.

The classroom was a disaster. It looked as if it had been vandalized, and I guess it had. Chairs and desks were in an incredible state of disarray. While the teacher talked, not a single student paid the slightest attention to him. They talked openly to each other, they turned their backs to him, walked around the room, laughed loudly, threw things, and while he read from the textbook, no one in the class even had theirs open.

My son was an integral part of the chaos.

When the dismissal bell rang, the students stampeded into the hallway – milling, shouting, and shoving like corralled cattle. Fortunately for me, I am rather large and probably somewhat intimidating to fourth graders, so they parted around me like an avalanche around a ponderosa pine. The fact that I collared the first little scoundrel who stepped on my freshly shined boots and threatened to thrash him soundly probably had a sobering effect on the rest of them.

My son – who had no idea that I was coming – stopped short when he saw me, and the "caught in the act" look on his face further convinced me that I had done the right thing. I told him to wait in the hall until I was through and that we would ride home together.

I introduced myself to the teacher. He was still sitting behind his desk, with an expression of apology, bewilderment, and relief all mixed together – he had *survived* another day. I again expressed my concern about my son. He said that my son was doing pretty well academically, especially *compared to the others,* and he produced his grade book to prove it. He said that my son's behavior was no worse than most, and better than many, and that all in all –

I had nothing to worry about.

When I expressed my horror at what I had witnessed through the window, he explained in some detail that this particular class of fourth graders had been "hellions" since kindergarten and that no one had ever been able to do anything with them – he had quit trying. He told me that I had simply been unfortunate to have a fourth grader instead of a third or fifth.

I listened as patiently as possible, but finally I said, "Mr._____, you need very badly to understand one thing. I am concerned with only one student in your class – and in this school for that matter – and that is my son. His behavior and his achievements are not to be measured by any standards other than those of his family, his religion, and his personal capabilities. My son's behavior in your class is reprehensible, his lack of respect for your position is intolerable, his academic achievement is shameful, and I hold you *personally responsible* for allowing this situation to develop, for tolerating it, and for not informing me about it. You will see an immediate change in my son's behavior and attitude – that is my *responsibility.* I will expect a regular report from you about his progress – that, and the behavior and respect of the rest of these students, is *your responsibility."*

This teacher had abdicated. He had signed a contract, given his word, and accepted pay to be a teacher – with all the inherent duties and obligations that that implies – and now, when things were tough, he refused to accept responsibility for his failures and blamed the outcome on former teachers, parents, and his students.

I get so discouraged with parents who blame all of their children's problems on public education, society, the church, the environment, the government, or some new medical analysis. When people elect to have children, they make a covenant that obligates them to a position of total *personal responsibility* for those children – for every aspect of what it means to grow from infancy to maturity – for their morals, their manners, their attitudes, their academic achievement, their intellectual and imaginative stimulation, and for their spiritual foundations. Listen to God's instructions to the parents of Israel:

> "These words which I command you this day
> shall be upon your heart; and
> *you* shall teach them diligently
> to your children."
> —Deuteronomy 6:6–7 RSV

Who is responsible?

You are.

Which Kind Are You?

"Two men went up to the temple to pray,
one a Pharisee and the other a tax collector."
—Luke 18:10 NIV

Which one are you?

One night after church, Judi needed a few things from the store. We went to the local grocery store, and because it was totally dark and raining lightly, I dropped her off at the front door. I parked where I could see both store exits so that when she came out, I could pick her up. For this time of night, there were a lot of shoppers. I opened my window about three inches to keep it from fogging.

There was a Chevy station wagon parked pretty close to me, and as I waited, the family who owned it came out. They had their sacks of groceries in a shopping cart. There were five of them. The husband and wife were about thirty-five — he was pudgy and balding; she was sort of plain vanilla — except her hair. The rain and gentle glow of the vapor lights in the parking lot caused it to shine nice and soft, and it curled all over her head and neck and down onto her face. I wanted to tell her how pretty it was, but I didn't. They had a boy — about ten, I guess. He was pushing the cart. He looked about right — jeans, T-shirt, and Reeboks. There were two nondescript others — about four and six, maybe, but their gender will forever remain a mystery.

The father opened the tailgate of the station wagon, and he and the boy unloaded the cart. When they finished, the father said, "Run the cart over there to the collection area, Danny."

As I said, it was raining — not hard, though — it wasn't offensive — just sort of a warm, pleasant drizzle that makes you want a good book, a fire, someone you love, and the leisure to be drowsy.

The boy didn't want to do it. They were about forty yards from me. I could hear them plainly, but I'm sure they never noticed me.

"Aw, Dad, it's raining," he complained.

"It will only take a second, and it won't hurt you." But there was no conviction in his voice. The father was reasoning with the boy — treating him as an equal —

and the boy took full advantage.

"Those people over there didn't put theirs back," he argued, pointing to several carts carelessly left in various places.

"We're not responsible for them, just for us," the father rejoined.

"But who cares?" the boy replied. "They got people hired to come out here and collect these carts."

The mother, tired of waiting, now joined in on the boy's side. "For heaven's sake, Carl, come on! One more cart in the parking lot won't change the history of the world."

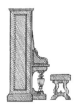

The boy sensed victory, he quickly pushed the cart to one side and opened the door to get in. The father shrugged his shoulders in defeat, moved to the driver's door, and put his hand on the door handle. Then he stopped. At first I couldn't figure out why, but I followed his eyes across the misty parking lot, and I saw what he saw – an elderly couple, her arm in his, slowly pushing their cart toward the collection area. It caused a whole transformation in him. His posture straightened, his chin lifted, and his shoulders squared a little. I suspect he looked much like the man he had been when he got married. And when he spoke, there was firmness and authority in his voice. "Danny," he said, "come here."

Danny didn't *hesitate,* and Danny didn't *argue* –

Fathers

♦

49

Danny came.

"Do you see those carts that are *in* the cart collection area? There are two kinds of people, Danny – those who put their carts away and those who don't. In this family, we put our carts away, because that's the kind of people we are. Don't ever forget that, Danny. Now put that cart where it belongs."

As the boy directed the cart to its appropriate place, it occurred to me how right the father was. There are two kinds of people in every area of life – two kinds of people – two kinds of fathers.

Which kind are you?

This Is My Son

"When Israel was a child, I loved him,
and out of Egypt I called my son.
The more I called them,
the more they went from me;
they kept sacrificing to the Baals,
and offering incense to idols.
Yet it was I who taught Ephraim to walk,
I took them up in my arms;
but they did not know that I healed them.
I led them with cords of human kindness,
with bands of love.
I was to them like those who lift infants to their cheeks.
I bent down to them and fed them. . . .
My people are bent on turning away from me. . . .
How can I give you up, Ephraim?
How can I hand you over, O Israel? . . .
My heart recoils within me;
my compassion grows warm and tender."
—Hosea 11:1–4, 7–8 NRSV

We were on our way to take our oldest son to college for the first time. We had decided to combine the trip with a brief vacation and visit some dear friends we had not seen in some time. We drove to the school, eight hundred miles away, dropped off his car and all of his possessions, and continued on our way. It was a happy, carefree time. We had been singing together since the children were small, and as we drove, we rehearsed our entire repertoire of songs over and over.

Our visit passed – much too quickly – and now we found ourselves returning to the college where we would leave our firstborn. The closer we got, the quieter it became. The singing stopped, and our words were tense and apprehensive. It really began to dawn on us that our family was breaking up for the very first time –

and that things would never again be the same.

The time came. We dreaded it – wanted to avoid it – but it came. We stood in the college parking lot beside his car – embarrassed, grieving, and silent. Everybody was waiting for me to say the right thing – but there are no right things at moments like that – and the silence was unbearable.

Finally, I said, "Well, I guess this is it, son. Say good-bye to your sister." I tried to keep the huskiness from my voice, but it was useless. They were a little awkward, but they embraced and she cried.

"Say good-bye to your brother." It was a lot easier for those two boys who had fought and argued. They held each other as though they had always been best of friends – but they didn't cry.

"Say good-bye to your mother." My voice was a raspy whisper now – I had lost control. His mother was already crying – had been crying for twenty minutes – and now he could hold it in no longer. He cried and held his mother for a long time.

Fathers

♦

52

And then it was my turn. He put his arms around my neck, and he said,

"I love you, Dad."

The finest words a man ever heard – the words that pay for the sleepless nights, the "loan" that never got repaid, the gas tank that never got refilled, the bed that never got made, the grass that never got mowed, the garbage that never got dumped. They pay for the thoughtlessness, the ring in the tub, the unfulfilled promise to "do it as soon as I get back," and all the lessons he promised he had learned – but had not.

"I love you, Dad."

That pays for it all, because what else is there? *What else could pay?* What else would stay in your heart? What else could you take to your hospital bed and to your death? "I love you, Dad." That will last. You can spend some of that every day for the rest of your life, and your account will be larger when you die than when that first "I love you" opened it – because the *interest* paid on love is very high

and always exceeds any withdrawals.

When it was done – when there was nothing to do but leave – we drove slowly away. I was leaving my son in the hands of strangers, in a strange city. As we drove from the campus, I had an overwhelming urge to stop and get out. I wanted to stand in the middle of the lawn and scream at the buildings, "This is my son! Do you know what that means to me? I'm leaving him here with you. This is my son. What happens to him, happens to me. What you do to him, you do to me. Please respect him and take care of him."

God gave this precious insight into His own feelings when Jesus was born in Bethlehem of Judea. The great star, the heavenly choir, the wise men, the shepherds, the angels who appeared – these were all his way of announcing to the world – "This is my Son! I'm leaving Him here with you. Please honor and respect Him. And remember – what you do to Him, you do to

Me." This affirmation is repeated at the baptism of Jesus, again at the transfiguration, and finally at the Cross. Each time, the voice of the Father affirms, "This is my Son. I'm proud of him, and I acknowledge him as my Son, my only begotten. Respect him."

An integral part of knowing God is understanding his feelings. He feels as we do, for we are made in his image. His feelings are separated from ours in degree, and they are not flawed by the flesh – but God grieves just as we grieve, he feels separation just as we do, and restoration fills his great heart just as it fills ours.

What do I want from my children in the final analysis? I want them to love me – nothing else will satisfy. Yes, of course, I want them to respect me and obey me –

but unless they love me,
their respect and their obedience is empty.

If my son offered me a check for a half-million dollars and said, "There, Dad, now we're even," I know what I would say. I'd say, "Son, you and I are *never* going to be even – you haven't got enough to get even with me. You'll *never* have enough. If you think you can pay for what your mother and I have invested in you with *money* – you've got a lot to learn about love." It was love that created the universe, it was love that created man, it was love that gave us a choice, and it was love that said we must die because we chose wrongly. It was love that created endless possibilities for everlasting life by sending Jesus to die for us – and there is only one acceptable response to God's love.

"Love the Lord your God with all your heart
and with all your soul and with all your mind.
This is the first and the greatest commandment."
—Matthew 22:37 NIV

God will never be satisfied with anything less than love, and everything else is less than that because love is the greatest thing of all.

"I love you, Dad."

Will He Give Him a Stone?

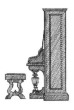

"Or what man is there of you, whom
if his son asks for bread, will he
give him a stone?"
—Matthew 7:9 KJV

It's funny how things work out – special things – things you would never think to ask for, things you couldn't possibly plan for. And if you're not careful, you don't even realize that a special gift has been sent your way, and so you miss much of the blessing.

I took my last two children to Lubbock, Texas, for college. It's a thousand miles from Montgomery to Lubbock. One was a senior, but had never been away from home; the other, a freshman – our baby – the last. The last one is like the first one – but different too. My excuse for going was that I needed to haul their stuff – which was enough to fill at least one freight car. But it was more than that – I wanted to hang on to them – even for just two or three more days. I was buying time.

The inevitable good-bye was a constant oppression.

We arrived Monday afternoon, and they got settled. On Tuesday evening, I told them I would pick them up at 8:30 Wednesday morning to help them start registration, then I was going to head home. But the thought of saying good-bye to them the next day kept me from sleeping Tuesday night, so I got up and wrote each of them a note. It was still dark when I went to the place they were staying. I pinned the note to the door – and left.

I haven't run from many things in my life – there were many times when I should have and didn't – but I ran from this one – I just couldn't do it.

Slowly – tearfully and alone – I drove away.

It's forty miles to Post from Lubbock, and before I got there, the sun had begun to rise. It doesn't rain often in West Texas. If you listen to the farmers, it rains like most folks go to church – Christmas and Easter – but it was raining when I left. For those of you not familiar with West Texas, I must explain something. Those of you who do know West Texas can skip this part. West Texas is flat. The most conspicuous – the most striking – the most absolutely mind-boggling, eye-blinking aspect of the landscape is its amazing *flatness.* You can see much of the world from West Texas. People who live there think you can see *all* of it. The names of the towns will help you understand the area. Read these names slowly: Brown-field, Shallow-water, Post, Little-field, Earth, Plain-view, Level-land, White-face, Ropes-ville, Pan-handle. These are graphic names. The people who originated them were honest, God-fearing folks who wouldn't tell a lie. But back to my story!

Driving to Post, off to my left (to the east), without a single obstruction except for a few oil derricks, was a glorious sunrise – as clear, as totally unclouded as anything you can imagine. Off to my right (to the west), over fields of cotton stretching as far as your imagination will carry you, was a driving rainstorm. In between, ascending in a high arc from north to south, from horizon to horizon – was a rainbow. I want to use some adjectives; I want to say that it was brilliant, spectacular, magnificent – none of them will do. In fact, it was a *double* rainbow. One was absolutely clear, with distinct and unmistakable colors; the other, its shadow, was misty and vague. I could see both ends – from ground to ground. I stopped, got out, and just looked. I tried to take pictures, but I couldn't get all of it – not even with a wide-angle lens.

It isn't easy to put in words – but I felt God's presence – if you had been there, I know you would have felt it too. I felt that God – my Father – was laying His hand on my shoulder; I felt as if I heard Him say, "I know how you feel, John. I had to say good-bye to My Son too. It nearly broke My heart. I felt your pain this morning, and I decided you might like this 'going away' present – from me to you. Lots of other folks will enjoy it, but really, I made it just for you."

And then it was gone.

One minute it was there – the next it was gone – without a trace. It will live in my heart and mind forever.

What an insight that rainbow provided me into the nature of divine fatherhood, and what an example for earthly fathers.

My children awoke fully expecting me to be there – instead they found a note.

> Dearest Brendan and Kristen,
>
> I know that you will be a little disappointed and a whole lot perplexed to learn that I have returned to Montgomery. My reasons for going without saying good-bye you will not understand until you have children of your own – but I just couldn't do it this time. I had a couple of things to say to you before I left, and I knew that the emotional distress of the moment would probably prevent me from saying them. I hope you know how deeply I love you and what great hopes I have for you. This is a learning time for both of

Fathers

♦

us. I must learn to give you up, and you must learn to make decisions without me. I pray that the morals, values, and spiritual principles that your mother and I have tried to instill in you will serve you well. I pray that your memories of home are good ones and that they will sustain you when the bad times come. Mom and I will pray for you every day – we are missing you already.

Dad

I believe that my absence conveyed more than my presence could have. I believe that my simple note of love and understanding communicated in a far more lasting way my feelings for them. Never underestimate the power of words communicated in writing.

I responded to my children's needs with an unexpected token of love and assurance, because I possessed a deeper wisdom and saw a larger picture than they had ever known or seen. God responded to my prayers with an unexpected token of love and assurance, because He possessed a deeper wisdom and saw a much bigger picture than I did. I had prayed for strength, for faith, and assurance – and He answered my prayer in the shape of a rainbow.

I wonder how many times I have asked for healing and missed the medicine. I wonder how many times I have pouted and doubted because I thought He didn't care – when the real problem was with my eyes, my ears, and my heart.

It is every father's obligation to constantly see a bigger picture than his children see and to react according to his wisdom, not theirs. In so doing, he gently opens their eyes to what he sees.

"If you then, being evil,
know how to give good gifts to your children,
how much more shall your Father who is in heaven
give what is good to those who ask Him!"
—Matthew 7:11 NASB

Just the Two of Us

It was just the two of us this time. It was much different from the first time – there were five of us, then – and it was our first trip. We had never been here before – that first time – when we brought our firstborn, and he was a son. This town – the campus – the buildings – and this airport where I sit awaiting my flight – were all strange to us – that first time.

This time, it was the last one – our baby – and she is a *girl* – and there is *much* difference. Oh – she's been here before (this is her junior year), but it was different this time. Before, her older brother was here, but now she will be here alone –

it was just the two of us this time.

We drove a thousand miles together – she and I. She was excited – I was not – but you don't send your baby girl alone – in a car – for a thousand miles, no, not in this world – you just don't do that. Her mother works, her brothers work, so it was me – I don't work; I preach – and her. We left at night, and we drove a thousand miles.

At first I drove – because it's mostly two-lane highways through small, southern towns. I drove and we talked. It was father, advisor – daughter, advisee – talk. We talked about all kinds of things – things I had planned to talk about – and it was serious. She listened patiently, agreed, disagreed – she tried to understand. She's twenty now – grown – and we haven't always been friends – in fact – although we have *loved* each other fiercely, we have not *liked* each other – often.

We are too much alike to like each other.

After we talked about the serious things, we fell silent. It wasn't that we didn't communicate – we just didn't talk. We rode in silence for hundreds of miles. She dozed, I dozed, but mostly we were awake, and we were very aware of each other and of what we were doing.

The town is familiar now – the buildings are like old friends. We know the instructors and administrators, and we know the politics, problems, and potentials. This is a good place for her – I am glad it exists. I feel good about her being here, and it delights me that she is so happy.

The past summer was hard on both of us. She did not enjoy being home. There were no friends, no activities, her job was boring, her evenings were lonely, and she was often unhappy. She tried – so did we – she really tried to be satisfied with us, but the time has come – her time – and we both knew it. She told me she was sorry about the summer – she said she really loved us – "but," she said – yes, dear God – "but." It is that time. She does love us – but it is her time, and love does not save us from growing up – though it is the greatest thing of all.

It was different this time. She is the last; I will not do this again – and dear God, I *want* to do this again. Her time has come – and my time too – but I know what time it is –

and she does not.

She drove me to the airport. As we drove, we were mostly quiet, and when we did talk – it was *small talk*. At the really important times, you can never think of the things you want to say anyway. I asked her not to come in and wait for my plane. I knew I would cry – and I hate to appear foolish in public. We parked in front of the terminal; I got out and got my bags. She got out too. We stood close and looked at each other – the look said much and our eyes filled, and then we held each other for a long time.

"I'll be all right Dad," she said to reassure me.

"I know," I said, "that's not the problem – that's not it at all. You don't understand – you can't right now. It's not your fault – it's just time."

"I love you, Dad," she said.

"I love you too," I said. We did not mean the same thing, but it was good, and it will last – because we do.

And then it was time.

She got in the car, and as I stood there and watched her drive away, I raised my hand in a final farewell. I remembered a cool, early September morning in 1958 – I was getting into my '54 Ford convertible, and my father was standing on that old, rickety, wooden back porch there on Rochester Road – just watching me, as I backed out of the driveway – heading for college. He raised his hand in a final farewell as I pulled away. It was *time* that he was watching, and now I was watching it.

When I walked into the terminal, I found myself singing some strains from an old Jim Croce song, "Time in a Bottle."

"If I could save time in a bottle. . . .
If words could make wishes come true,
I'd save every day like a treasure and then,
Again, I would spend them with you."

And that's what it is – it's *time*. Solomon said, "There is a time for everything." He was right, and that shouldn't surprise us. He also said that most folks main problem is that they don't know what time it is – they're always running around in circles when it's time to stand still. God is always trying to get us to see what time it is, but we are far too busy or careless or insensitive – besides, we often do not wish to know. You can't save time in a bottle – that's the rub – you can't. You can only know what time it is.

There is a time when being a father
is the most important thing to do.

You can't postpone it. It won't wait for you – there is no next year in fathering. One day you wake up and they're grown and gone.

Do you know what time it is – in your life?

Fathers

ℋ

◆

59

Time in a Bottle

I finished the last story by saying that you can't save time in a bottle – maybe I was wrong. You know, it's the most amazing thing how your mind works. The morning after I wrote that story down, I woke up thinking about Fred Alexander. I couldn't figure out why. I've only seen Fred two or three times in the last thirty years. I lay there in bed and puzzled over it – did I have a dream about Fred that I couldn't remember? And then it came to me. I don't know how or why, but it came to me –

as clearly as a sunrise.

We were at Michigan Christian College, and it was the spring of 1961. The school year had just ended, finals were over, dorm rooms were empty, annuals signed, cars loaded, good-byes said – we were going home. There were seven or eight of us left – as I remember it – Wayne Baker, John Losher, Jim Began, Bill Hall, Bob Forrester, John Whitwell, Gary . . . something, myself, and Fred Alexander.

We were the only ones left.

We met in one of the now empty, bare, sterile dorm rooms. Fred Alexander was a school administrator of sorts, and he also served as the chorus director. He and his wife, Claudette, were much loved by the students.

We met by design – one of the boys had specifically set up the meeting and had invited Fred. We met to say good-bye – in some final, official, personal way. Each of us tried to say something important – significant. We tried to find an expression for what was in our hearts – to give vent to the love, the sorrow, the loneliness that we felt.

We were so aware of time.

Until now, we had not been aware at all. We had played football and basketball in the long fall afternoons. We had eaten in the cafeteria, gone to chapel, dated the girls, talked late at night about unimportant things, gone to Red Knapps for hamburgers, played Spades and Hearts, crammed for tests, bragged about our adventures, and fooled away endless hours canoeing on the Clinton River and visiting Yates Cider Mill – all with no consciousness of time; but we were conscious now – painfully so. But time does not need consciousness to pass. The year was over – we were older and wiser – things had changed without our notice.

They would never be the same again.

The meeting was awkward; we were embarrassed. We were only boys, and we were experiencing things for the first time, so we had no words for our feelings. Although I was some older than the other boys, I was as lost as any of them, maybe more so, because growing up had come very slowly to me.

Finally, we joined hands in a circle – and we prayed. And as we prayed, we began to cry – first one – then another – finally all. It was a new experience for some of us. When we finished our prayer, we shook hands – then, awkwardly we embraced each other –

and then it was time to go.

We asked Fred if he had something to share with us. His eyes were red – I don't think he was much used to crying either. His voice shook, but I remember what he said.

"If I could have any wish right now, I'd wish that I could take this moment and put it in a jar – and put a lid on it, so each of us could hold it. And every now and then – wherever we go – at those special times when life is cruel and we need it so badly – we'd open the jar and let a little bit of what is in this room out – and we would remember the experience of loving and being loved –

and it would make us whole again."

He may have said more, but that's what I remember. Oh, my dear brother Fred — how I need that jar today. I do remember that moment, and writing about it has been just like opening the jar.

I don't know — maybe I was wrong.

Maybe you *can* save time in a bottle.
Maybe you *can* preserve the loving.
Maybe remembering is as good as being there.
No, you can't *go* back, but you can *be* back.
Maybe you can save time in a bottle.

That's what makes it all worthwhile. That's what you get for *being there* — for struggling, for sacrificing, for raising them — you get precious memories —

and so do your children.

Memories are sustaining things; they give meaning and purpose — not only to the past but to the present — and they bring hope for the future.

Reach up and take that jar off the shelf. Open the lid slowly – don't let too much escape at once. Savor every aroma and draw strength for today from the memories of the past.

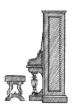

"Precious memories, how they linger,
How they ever flood my soul.
In the stillness of the midnight,
Precious sacred scenes unfold."
—J. B. F. Wright

Fathers

♦

T H R E E

Why Is Love So Hard?

Love means giving
the answer that is *best*
for the one you love
and never sacrificing
long-term good for
short-term happiness.

Why Is Love So Hard?

The apostle Paul says that love is the greatest thing of all, and most folks would agree, I think. But if, indeed, it is the greatest thing, why don't things work out better? Why is there so much disappointment, pain, and heartache in family relationships?

I mean, we all love each other,
don't we?

When I talk about love, I don't mean love as in "falling in love" or as in loving your truck or chocolate pie — that comes easy and natural. I mean love as in "God so loved the world that He gave His Son," or "Husbands love your wives as you love yourself." That kind of love doesn't come naturally — you have to work at it. Falling in love is the most primitive and unrealistic form love has — but it's the one we talk about most — and sing about, read about, and watch on TV — and it's the one we want most, because it comes naturally and it's so easy — so delicious and tingly. The problem is that we expect "being in love" to be the same way —

and it's not.

Loving is hard because it isn't always reciprocated — or understood for that matter — and when it's not, you can't just walk away like in falling in love. Loving folks — even children — doesn't mean they will return your love or appreciate it. And you can't make them, no matter how hard you try. Children often say, "If you loved me, you would . . . say 'yes' to me." They say this because, to them, love means that you do what they want.

Love is hard because it makes you say no, when everything inside you wants to say yes. Love is hard because it makes you say yes, when everything inside you wants to say no. Love is hard because it risks alienation and is sometimes misunderstood. Love is hard because it will not risk long-term good for short-term appreciation. Love is hard because it acts according to its own principles. Love is hard because it makes us behave well when we want to behave badly. Love persists in seeking the good of the beloved —

not as the beloved wants,
but as love dictates.

67

The following brief and painful illustration will serve well to demonstrate my point. I was a musically talented child, born into a musically talented family. Somewhere, about the age of ten or eleven, my mother decided that I should learn to play the piano. She made great personal sacrifices to provide the instrument and money for lessons.

I hated it – resisted it – fought, argued, pouted, and was so thoroughly obstinate that I finally wore her down and she let me quit. What I would give today if her love had been tougher. She settled for short-term peace, purchased at the cost of long-term good. Her love for me was flawed by her failure to respond to her own wisdom and experience. She wanted to save herself and me from the pain of insisting on what was best. She failed to realize that living through the rejection created by an unwanted answer forms the foundation for leaping to a higher level of loving – one not based on getting what I want. Those who avoid that rejection do so only temporarily and are doomed to experience love only at its lowest, most unrewarding level.

In the gospel of John, chapter 15, Jesus instructs His disciples to "love each other as I have loved you." How does Jesus love us? Let me call your attention to a single chapter in Matthew's gospel – chapter 25. It is divided into three sections – the Parable of the Ten Virgins, the Story of the Talents, and the Vision of Judgment. In each story there is a happy ending and a sad ending. Jesus welcomes five of the virgins, the five- and two-talented men, and the sheep into the joy of salvation. He sends the other five of the virgins, the one-talented man, and the goats into eternal condemnation. Does Jesus love all the virgins, all the talented men, and the goats as well as the sheep? It is inadmissible that he does not. Which of His responses is the loving one? Is the heart of Jesus untouched by the pleas of the lost? Jesus loves us enough to say yes and to say no, and we must love each other as He has loved us.

No aspect of life appears easier and turns out to be more difficult than that of loving the people who are important to us. We think that it will come naturally to us, but in reality –

we must work harder at loving
than at anything else.

Kane

He was just a fat little bundle of loose skin covered with yellow-gold hair when we got him. It was the only time I ever paid money for a dog – a lot of money – one hundred twenty-five dollars to be exact. It was precious money – money I couldn't afford to spend – but it was Christmas, and the puppy was sort of a family Christmas present. He was a yellow Labrador retriever, and we named him Kane.

He was beautiful. Even when he was small and clumsy, tripping over his own – too big for his body – feet, he was beautiful. As he grew and filled the folds of his too large skin, he was a joy to us. When he ran, his powerful muscles rippled under that golden coat, and he reminded me of a young lion. He went everywhere with us. He loved the water, he would retrieve anything, and he was gentle with the children and with friends.

He wasn't very smart. In fact, he was unbelievably stupid. He would have starved to death if we hadn't guided him to his food dish. Teaching him tricks was out of the question, but he was loyal to us, and he was ours –

and we loved him.

My sons and I built him a large pen. We lived in Kingman, Arizona, at the time, and the boys and I went out to an old, abandoned mining shaft near Cerbat. We worked like dogs, digging out a twelve-by-twelve timber for a corner post and some six-by-sixes. We stretched and nailed some hurricane fencing, which a neighbor had given us, around the posts. It didn't look like much, but it did the job of keeping Kane at home when we were gone.

One day, when Kane was nearly a year old, he ran into the road in front of our house to retrieve something the children had thrown, and he was hit by a UPS truck.

They called me at work. I came home immediately and found everyone in tears. They had taken him to the veterinarian. He wasn't dead, but it would have been better if he had been. The vet told me that Kane's shoulder was shattered, two of his legs were broken, and he had serious internal injuries. He said he could set the legs, put steel pins in his shoulder, and operate to stop the hemorrhaging. It would cost five hundred dollars, and he couldn't guarantee that the dog would live.

I didn't have five hundred dollars. I didn't have fifty. I guess I could have placed some things at risk and borrowed it, but I had a decision to make — one that involved the children's education and our shaky financial future. I decided I couldn't do it. Everything inside me wanted to save the dog. I wanted to say yes — I wanted to go home and tell my kids that I had saved the day. I wanted to be a hero —

but I had to say no.

I told the vet to put Kane to sleep, and I went home to explain to my children why Kane had to die. We sat around the kitchen table, and the children listened with white, tear-stained faces and large, unblinking eyes. It isn't easy, you know. How much is a dog's life worth? Children have no way of measuring the value of their dog's life against money. Children only know that they love their dog, and that somehow their father's financial failures mean that their dog has to die. It isn't easy to love a father who fails — who doesn't pull the rabbit out of the hat when the chips are down. It is a tribute to my children that they tried to understand what I didn't understand; they tried to trust me and to love me.

When I had explained it to them, they asked no questions — they knew their father. The middle-age boy got up and went to his room; in a few minutes he returned with his bank. In it was his life savings — money he had been saving for two years doing odd jobs to buy a motorcycle. He spilled the contents out on the table — fifteen dollars in pennies, nickels, dimes, and quarters — and said that he would gladly spend it all to save his dog.

I tried to explain the difference between fifteen dollars and five hundred — but a child measures value differently from an adult. It's not the amount —

it's the heart. When you give everything you have — it has to be enough. I said I appreciated what he wanted to do, but it didn't change things. The children went to their rooms to cry out their grief, and I walked outside. I thought I was going to explode with frustration and anger at my helplessness. I found a stick that Kane had been retrieving for us, and I walked over to the empty pen that had been built with so much care and hope.

I began whacking that twelve-by-twelve corner post with the stick, and I began to cry and to pour out my anguish. My wife came out — her eyes red with tears from consoling the children. "John," she said, "what's wrong?"

"It's hell to be poor," I said. "I love my kids as much as any man, and I loved the dog — more than I wanted to. I try to live right and do right —

but right now I hurt so bad
I could die."

It was a long time ago, but remembering it, and writing about it, has brought back the ache and the anguish. I did the right thing. I knew it then and I know it now.

But doing the right thing is seldom easy,
and loving is very hard.

❧

To My Daughter

I have preached many funerals, waited by the bedside of the terminally ill, counseled hundreds of emotionally disturbed families, and held the hands of parents whose children had committed suicide or serious crimes or were drug addicted. I have dealt with sexual perversion, alcoholism, loneliness, and depression. But none of those things produced a greater depth of despair than when I prayed and counseled with a grieving father and helped him formulate the following letter. The circumstances you can piece together from its content; the details are too lengthy and personal to recount.

I do feel compelled to add this disclaimer: This is a last-resort letter. It is the culmination of months of intensive struggle and heartache. Every conceivable attempt to compromise, to reach an understanding, to find some common ground, had been exhausted. A time came when a stand had to be taken, when compromise would only prolong the agony and postpone the inevitable.

Dear Melissa,

I received your letter three days ago, but I thought it best to wait to respond until I had opportunity to consider your request and to pray. Your decision to proceed with the marriage, as you know, is against my every wish. You have stated once again all your reasons for your decision. I find nothing that we have not been over before, and I repeat that your very reasons display your immaturity and the completely false notions you have about the step you are taking. I sympathize deeply with your feelings of frustration, loneliness, and emptiness; but that does not change the fact that you are making a tragic mistake by trying to solve your problems — and Kent's, too — by marriage.

Melissa, you have asked me to participate in the wedding and to "give you away." I simply cannot, in good conscience, do that. In fact, I have pledged myself not to encourage this marriage in any way. I will not be at your wedding. I realize that I cannot rectify my failure to take a stand on previous occasions by taking one now, but I also realize that giving in one more time cannot be justified by my former cowardice and vacillation.

I'm sure this will make you angry with me. It is useless to plead — as you have pled with me on a thousand other occasions, successfully. It is my prayer that some day you will understand that I have acted more in harmony with my love for you in this case than I have in those others where I gave in to you. If you have any honor in your heart for me as your father, you will know what this is costing me. Perhaps that will help you understand how serious an error I believe you are committing and how earnestly I am seeking to help you avoid a tragedy so cataclysmic that you will be scarred for life by the consequences.

I know you are unaware that your mother and I made the same mistake. We carried the burden of it for twenty years, and it finally became more than we could bear. Your unhappy, insecure teenage years were the result of the constant tension between your mom and me. We tried to hold our marriage together for you and your brothers. I'm glad we did – it was far better than the alternatives – but I hope you can see the misery it caused for all of us. Both our parents warned us against it, but they lacked the moral fiber to say no and to throw the weight of their absence and lack of support behind it. We might have married anyway, but at least they would have always known they had obeyed their convictions.

You have made a decision; it is your right to do so. And although I believe it to be a grievous error, I respect your right. I, too, have made a decision. My decision is based upon greater experience, wisdom, and specific knowledge. These decisions are in direct conflict; there is no middle ground – no room for compromise. I have listened to all your reasons; you have listened to mine. If you choose to proceed – you must proceed alone. You simply cannot have it both ways. You have had things your way for so long that I realize how terribly bewildering it must be to you to come up against a decision that you cannot change by pleading, shouting, pouting, or manipulating.

I do not know how this will affect our future relationship. It will always be between us, and we will pay a price for that. My attitude toward your marriage will not change after the wedding, but I have no wish to indefinitely close the door on our relationship. I will pray for you every day, and I sincerely hope you will pray for me. That will be our common ground for the immediate future. I do not hope that your marriage will fail so that I can be proven correct. You simply have no chance to succeed.

I love you more now than ever before. I have been so totally absorbed with my own problems these last years that I have failed miserably to give you the time and attention you needed. God forgive me for that. I need your forgiveness too. I stand ready to help – to advise – to do anything that will be to your good, and I will continue to stand ready after this marriage is finalized. If I make an error by being too hard in this one instance, God knows I have made a thousand errors by being too easy previously.

Words fail to express the grief I feel as I write this. I feel the despair that always accompanies failure and our inability to go back. God forgive me. I really do love you – if I didn't, sending this letter would not be tearing me apart.

Dad

Stories like this always ignite our curiosity, and we wonder – "What happened?" There are two points I want to make as I keep you in suspense about that. First, no matter how things turn out – it will not justify the sins that create the situation. Second, movie makers have the luxury of making their stories turn out as they wish – real life is seldom that way. We all want happy endings – unfortunately, we do not wish to pay the price that is required.

The marriage was postponed.

If you had asked this father at any point during his daughter's formative years if he loved her, his immediate and decisive answer would have been "Yes," and he would have believed that with all of his heart. If you had asked this father how he knew that he loved her, I'm sure his response would have been centered around the feeling of affection he had for her and the way he provided for her. What I want you to see is that neither his affection nor his providing led him to share practically and emotionally in his daughter's life. Their relationship was one of mutual manipulation, and they both paid a terrible price for it. They were strangers living in the same house. Love does not behave in that way. His love failed them because it did not build a trusting, respectful, and intimate relationship.

Every parent needs to see the implications of that. Thinking that you love someone – even saying it – does not mean that you do. Love must take on definition to be meaningful. If we do not act in a loving way –

love is just a word.

Son, Don't Go

Perhaps no more meaningful definition of love is given to us than in John's gospel.

"For God so loved the world,
that he gave his only begotten Son . . ."

We can't even imagine how much pain there was in that giving.

Love makes you hurt because it involves offering choices, and folks don't always choose what you want them to or what's good for them. The rest of the John 3 passage says,

> " . . . that whosoever believeth in him
> should not perish."
> —John 3:16 KJV

"Whosoever believes" means that God gives folks a choice. And when you sacrifice as much as he did to give people a choice and they choose wrongly – it really hurts.

Love is hard because it makes you hurt. God speaks through the prophet Hosea concerning his beloved people Israel.

> "I cared for you in the desert,
> in the land of burning heat.
> When I fed them, they were satisfied;
> when they were satisfied, they became proud;
> then they forgot me."
> —Hosea 13:5–6 NIV

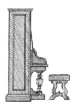

What a graphic tale of loneliness and despair is told in those words. It is a tale experienced by every parent – a tale of ingratitude, of love not reciprocated.

Love is hard because it makes you say yes, when everything inside of you wants to say no. Chapter 15 of Luke's gospel contains the treasured story of the prodigal son and the loving father. The son comes to the father and asks for his inheritance. The father knows why he wants it. The father *can* say no – he *wants* to say no – everything inside of him *tells* him to say no. Saying no would be the easiest thing to do. The father knows the perils of the world. He knows where the boy is going, and he knows what can happen there. He knows that sin is fun and that devotion to sensuality is both destructive and addictive. He knows that the boy may not ever come back – either because he has no desire or because he can't – death is a real possibility. The father knows all of the possible outcomes – but he also knows that there is no other way – and he says, "Okay, if that's what you really want."

The father gives him the money, and the boy packs his belongings and leaves. The father follows him down the driveway to the road and watches the boy's back as the distance between them grows. He wants to cry out – "Son, don't go! Son, don't go! Stay here with me – we'll work something out."

But he bears his grief in silence.

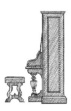

The son is totally unaware of his father. His excitement over getting out on his own — having his own apartment, selecting his own friends, getting up and going to bed whenever he wants, having no one to boss him around — the allurement of unrestrained sensual pleasure — the power of youth and plenty of money — all of these keep his attention focused on the road before him. He doesn't even turn around and wave. He doesn't know the pain that is in his father's heart; he doesn't know what love is —

but he's going to learn.

Love is hard because the answers aren't always the same. Loving means that you have to give the answer that is best for the one you love and that you never sacrifice long-term good for short-term happiness — that you never buy your own peace at the expense of the beloved's failure to achieve their maximum potential. Love risks personal loss and loneliness — even rejection.

Most of us don't love very well. We keep wanting it to be easy — we demand that it be easy — and when it's not, we walk away and call it something else. We need badly to remember that those who experience the heartache of rejection and doubt as they stand in the road and watch their children go — prove themselves worthy to experience the overwhelming joy that comes from standing in the same road and

seeing them come home.

Love

Nothing tests parental patience and skill more than their children's heady, bewildering experience of "falling in love." When they forget to eat, pay more attention to their hair than to what's on TV, spend more time brushing their teeth than eating, or ask you to buy a special kind of deodorant; when they don't want you to hear their phone conversations and don't want to tell you who called — you'll know it's "that time." It's the emotional roller-

coaster-of-exhilaration-and-pain time – the wild, unreasonable happiness
time, the cloud-nine time. And all of this causes complete short-term memory failure – they can't find their room, their shoes, or their head. They
either don't have the time or desire to eat or don't have the time or desire
to do anything but eat. They talk endlessly on the phone about absolutely

nothing – then forget to hang up. They believe everything they hear, except when their parents or anyone over thirty is talking.

Yes, it is that time.

Falling in love is the final act in losing innocence. Guiding a child through the emotional whirlwinds of "erotica" demands a sensitivity that will tap every parental resource. Because I had taught junior high school for so many years, I dreaded this time in my children's lives far more than even their learning to drive.

It is inconceivable to an early teen that their stodgy, outdated progenitors ever entertained romantic notions. Dad is bald and drives a station wagon; Mom is gray, overweight, and out of touch. They are both hopelessly dull – how could they possibly understand palpitations of the heart? That is why your child so often says with exasperation, "Oh, how could you possibly understand!"

Your major task is to first convince them that you do – not by saying you do – but by finding opportunities to tell them about the things you did during that time in your life.

And you must be honest.

Nobody is ever prepared for falling in love. How could you be? The experience comes upon you full blown, with no warning. I advise parents that a good sense of humor is invaluable. I do not mean that you should make fun of or belittle the seriousness of your child's feelings. I only mean that humor can add balance to the fleeting and ever changing emotions they undergo.

As long as things go well in boy-girl relationships, parents play a relatively minor role. But the inevitable *breaking up* and the devastation that follows are very real and nearly always bring a parent into the picture.

Losing innocence, and particularly falling in love, provides critical times for bonding parents and children. It only comes once – don't miss it. It is also a critical stage in spiritual development – a time when prayer and providence become practical and

a personal awareness of God
becomes a reality.

Parental Consent

We lived at 3524 Rochester Road in Royal Oak, Michigan. I was a freshman in high school, trying out for the football team. My coach had given me a parental permission form that my mother and father had to sign in order for me to play and a form to be filled out by a doctor, which said that I was healthy enough to be kicked, knocked down, beaten, and pounded mercilessly without causing permanent damage to my body.

I didn't want to take either form home. We were given a week to have them filled out and returned. I kept them both in my locker. After the week was up, every day before practice the coach would say, "The following people have not turned in their forms" – and he would read the list. At first, there were a lot of names on it, and it didn't bother me too much; but every day the list grew shorter, and my name became more and more conspicuous. Finally, there were only two names left – a Jehovah's Witness boy and me.

The coach called us in before practice on Wednesday and told us that if we didn't turn in the forms by Friday – he simply could not allow us to practice anymore. He was a very nice man, for a football coach – one of the most decent coaches I ever had. He asked us if there was a problem, and both of us were embarrassed, because we didn't want to talk about it. The Jehovah's Witness boy said that his parents' religious convictions were a major obstacle. The coach wanted us both to play – the Witness boy was a very promising player – so he told him he would talk to his parents.

I told him that my mother didn't know that I was practicing for football and that she was strictly opposed to my playing. I, also, very reluctantly told him that we had no money for me to get a physical from a doctor. It cost eight dollars – I still remember. He said that he had a friend who was a doctor and that he would take care of the physical –

but it was up to me to get my mother's signature.

Well, the worst possible thing happened in practice that afternoon. We were running a simple tackling drill designed to teach us how to knock the ball loose from the runner by using our helmets. Somehow, I caught my cheekbone right on the shoulder pad of the runner I was tackling. The collision removed a patch of skin about the size of a silver dollar. It really wasn't serious at all, but the red, raw, exposed flesh looked terrible.

My mother was working, and she didn't get home until 5:30 or 6:00, so it had been pretty easy to disguise my whereabouts after school. When I

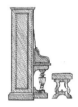

Why Is
Love So
Hard?

♦

came in the door, she was home. I had the forms in my hand and my speech ready, but I didn't get to give it.

"What happened to your face?" she said, and there was some urgency in her voice.

"I was playing football with some guys after school," I hedged – but it was sort of true.

"How many times have I told you not to play that game; it's just too rough."

"You've told me several times."

I didn't mention the forms. I went to my room and waited for my dad to get home.

After supper my dad always read the newspaper in the living room while my mother cleaned the kitchen. I took the parental consent form to him and explained that I needed his signature. Although my facial laceration had been quite a topic at supper, he took the form, told me to get a pen, and he signed it.

"I have to have Mom's signature too," I explained.

"Sure," he said. "Take it to her, and tell her I said to sign it." He returned to his newspaper.

I took it into the kitchen, explained briefly, and showed her where to sign. She got real upset, said she wasn't going to do any such thing, and that I must be crazy for asking her. I showed her where Dad had signed it and told her that he said that she should.

"Well," she said, "you can tell him that he must be crazy too."

I went back into the living room.

"She won't sign it," I said. He put the paper down.

"Did you tell her I said to?"

"Yes," I said.

"What did she say?"

"I don't think you want to know."

"I want to know what she said."

"She said that you must be crazy."

"Let me have that form," he said, and he put the paper down and got out of his chair.

"Yes, sir," I said.

He took the card and went into the kitchen. I followed, heart in my mouth. I didn't know what to expect, but what happened was certainly nothing I might have expected. My mother was standing at the sink with her back to us, moving the dishes around in the soapy water – she wasn't washing them –

she was just moving them around.

Why Is
Love So
Hard?

♦

80

Her shoulders were shaking, her eyes were closed, and she was crying. Big tears ran down her face and plopped in the dishwater. She wasn't sobbing or making noise, she was just crying, real quietly. I knew by the way she was crying – by the way her shoulders were slumped – that she was going to sign the form. She wasn't angry or defiant, she didn't have her teeth set and her shoulders squared for a fight. She had already given up. My dad knew it, too, and he walked over and placed both of his hands very gently on her shoulders.

"Florence," he said, "it's for the best. The boy's got to have a chance to prove himself."

"Oh, you men!" she said.

And there was a lot of disgust in her voice. I didn't understand it then and only understand a little of it now – but you wives and mothers out there – you know what "Oh, you men!" means.

Mom dried her eyes and her hands on her apron, and she took the form from my dad and sat down at the kitchen table. It was only a card table – one of those cardboard kind with the folding legs – in the tee-tiniest kitchen you can imagine. She sat down, and she read the form – every word. There were several clauses in there that could make a person apprehensive – who to contact in case of injury, was I allergic to any medication, the name of our family doctor, and where I should be sent if hospitalization were required – stuff like that. She picked up the pen, and then she started to cry again. I thought she had changed her mind, but she signed it –

and the tears splashed right on the form.

She looked up at me and said, "Go on! Go on – play football! Knock your teeth loose and break your nose – and for what? Well, I don't have to watch, and I won't." Then she put her face in her hands and *really* cried. But she didn't have to watch, and she never did.

That was a long time ago. I can still see the tee-tiny kitchen and my mother with her face in her hands and the tears splashing on the parental consent form. I can still see her drying her eyes on her apron – you know moms don't much wear aprons anymore; they just put real pretty ones on the kitchen wall to make it look "country," but they never put them on. I guess it's because of microwaves and automatic dishwashers – it's a great loss, because moms are often best remembered in their aprons. I can still hear her say,

"Oh, you men!"

I was learning about marriage and about mothers and fathers – and God too. I didn't mean to learn, and my parents didn't stage the scene in order to

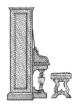

teach me a valuable lesson or create a memory, but I watched them love each other that evening – and me, too – because that's how love works. Only I didn't know that was love until much later when I took my oldest son's parental consent form to his mother for her signature. Some things never change – the doctor's fee had, and there was an additional insurance form – but his mother cried and said,

"Oh, you men!"

Why Is
Love So
Hard?

♦

82

FOUR

Coming of Age

She's not coming home
– we've lost our baby.
She's becoming what
we raised her to be.

Coming of Age

We try to remember when it happened for us – when the magic moment arrived when we knew. We all know that it happens – that there is a time of innocence and then there is a time of sin-consciousness – but when does it happen? When do we cross the line? What combination of age, experience, knowledge, awareness, physical maturity, and sensual sensitivity are required? Is it a moment of revelation? Is it a process?

What are the ingredients of accountability?

By accountability, I mean an awakening moral consciousness. A consciousness that has a spiritual and emotional quality inherent in it. A consciousness that recognizes those universal truths that define what it means to be human and to be responsible. An accountable person is one who not only is aware of the code, but of personal violations – aware of both the internal and external implications and aware of guilt and wrongdoing.

I heard a little story recently that may serve my point well. A mother, who was working in the kitchen, heard a piercing scream of agony from her five-year-old son who was playing in the bedroom with his two-year-old sister. When the mother went to investigate, she found that the sister, indignant over some sense of unfair play, had grabbed her brother's hair in both fists and was pulling with all her might. The mother, with much difficulty, finally succeeded in prying the little girl's death grip loose. The brother insisted that she be punished for her actions. The mother very carefully explained that the sister was so young and innocent that she didn't know that pulling someone's hair hurt, and so she wouldn't be punished. The brother was skeptical. No sooner had the mother returned to the kitchen than she heard another piercing wail – this time from the little sister. When she asked her son what had happened he said,

"She knows now."

My point would be that there is a wide difference, even now, in what the sister understands – what the brother understands – and what the mother understands – about pulling hair and pain. Those levels of understanding each have a corresponding level of accountability.

Coming
of Age

♦

C. S. Lewis said that he remembered the exact moment, the time, the place, and the circumstances of his coming of age, and I suspect that most of us could remember, if we really probed our past. I know when I became accountable. I do not say that I knew it then – I had no past to judge it against, and so I only knew that something had changed. I do not say that accountability came upon me full blown, like a bright lightening flash against a black sky. I do say that this event caused a shadow to fall across the clear, sunlit skies of my youth and innocence. I do say that after this incident, nothing was ever the same. Even though my todays were often sunny, happy, and thoughtless, my tomorrows had gray shadows of warning around the edges.

It seems critical to me that parents be sensitive to the telltale signs of the budding maturity we call puberty. I remember my first junior high teaching job. I noticed one of my girls with her head down on her desk, crying convulsively. I gave the class an assignment, went to her desk, and escorted her into the hallway. I was sure some cataclysmic tragedy had occurred. I soothed her and assured her that I was her friend and that she could tell me anything without fear. "Please tell me what's wrong," I urged.

She raised her reddened eyes to mine, looked me full in the face, and said, "I don't know."

And she didn't.

Nearly everything changes during that transition from the innocence of childhood to the accountability of adulthood. What once was humorous is now serious. What once was serious is now humorous. What once was punished severely and spontaneously is now discussed. Hormonal and attitudinal changes leave children totally bewildered by their own behavior. It is a time of emotional upheaval that questions everything, believes anything, remembers nothing, and is always changing.

They laugh or cry,
not knowing
or caring –
how or why.

Innocence Lost

Picture a street . . . ah, no, picture two streets running parallel. Between those two streets is an alley. Now, on either side of this alley, facing opposite directions, are two rows of houses. Have you got that? Now here's the hard part. One of the houses is missing. That space, where the house is missing, is called a – vacant – lot – because, dearly beloved –

it has no house.

This vacant lot had become a playground for all the neighborhood children. Tag, hide-and-seek, kick-the-can, fox-and-goose, and yes, even the national pastime – baseball – were all played upon this lot.

One fine, fall afternoon, about ten boys were gathered for a baseball game. They ranged in age from nine to thirteen. They wore old, black sneakers or were barefoot. Their T-shirts were dirty from the day's play, and their blue jeans (either it was before the advent of Levi's or we couldn't afford them) were worn, patched, or out at the knees. Their equipment consisted of a single baseball, whose cover had long since disappeared and been replaced by black electrical tape wound carefully round and round the strings of the ball. There was one bat – broken. It had three wood screws holding it together, and it too was taped. The bases were either newspapers or rags held in place by rocks. Since there was no first baseman or right fielder, the pitcher could get a first-base runner out from the pitcher's mound and any ball hit to right field was an automatic out.

The game was hotly contested; the lead had seesawed back and forth. No major league contest was ever played with more intensity. I was pitching. My friend David Moody, a year and half younger than I, was on the other team. David was not a very good player, and he was at bat.

He hadn't been on base all day. He had struck out, popped up, hit to right field, or had found some new, creative way to make an out. As I said, he was my friend. We had grown up together. His folks and mine had gone to church together time out of mind. They even went to dinner and played pinochle together. His older sisters, Audrey and Faye, were my sister's best friends.

Although the game was close, my team was ahead and I felt very benevolent toward David. I gave him a nice, soft pitch right down the middle. David promptly took advantage of my kindness and smacked the ball across the street, right into Mrs. Owen's rose bushes. He got all the way to second base. Maybe that's where the trouble started. I was miffed because

he had taken advantage of my generosity.

A couple of plays later, another boy got a hit, and David decided to further impress his teammates and score. It was a mistake. He was a very slow runner. My job as pitcher was to cover home plate. I had the ball, waiting to tag him out, fifteen feet before he ever got there. He knew he didn't stand a chance, but he decided to try the only option left to him. He charged me – which was another mistake. I was a whole head taller, thirty pounds heavier, and I saw him coming. Like I said, I guess it started when he hit my pitch so hard. I had the ball in my glove, and when he dove at me, head first, I just stepped back, and as he flew by, I hit him right in the face with my glove.

It sort of stunned him at first, but I could tell he was real upset. Everybody making fun of him didn't help, but then he made another mistake – worse than the first two. He decided to fight. I just made fun of it at first. When he tried to hit me, I just ducked or warded off his blows. He really got mad then. I guess he sort of went crazy, and I couldn't stop him from hitting me some, and I started to get upset myself. I pleaded with him to stop, but he was like a human tornado. Finally, he hit me right on my ear and I got mad – really mad. I hit him on the nose and knocked him down. Then I jumped on him, pinned his arms to the ground with my knees and proceeded to slap his face with my open hand. Back and forth – back of my hand, palm of my hand – I slapped him. The other boys had made a circle around us and were yelling encouragement to both of us –

which wasn't much help to either of us.

When I began to come to myself, when the light of reason began to filter through my red brain, I looked down and saw the face of my friend, David Moody. It was covered with blood from his nose and mouth. I was absolutely horrified by what I was doing. It was against everything I had ever been taught. I was not by nature a bully and normally avoided fights of any kind. I didn't even like to watch.

I jumped up, and I began to run. I raced down the alley into an intersecting alley, down it to the street, across the street, and into another vacant lot, which was across from my house. I was so overcome by the course of events that I knelt there and began to cry.

I hadn't even realized that David was following me. Still angry, bent on vengeance, he came to where I was and found me kneeling and crying. He stood behind me for a moment, then stooped down and put his arms around me; and he, too, began to cry as though his heart would break.

Picture it if you will, two boys – one eleven, the other thirteen – arms around each other, crying in a vacant lot – their first real dawning consciousness of wrongdoing –

of having violated some sacred injunction.

True to our teaching, our heritage, we begged forgiveness. We made a pact, as boys will, to ever be friends and to never allow anything to separate us. The pact worked. We never fought again or even had cross words. I'm sorry to say that it wasn't due to our fidelity or our characters. David Moody died about a month later in a drowning accident. I remember his funeral, and I remember thinking when the preacher was talking that he didn't know David very well. I wished they would let me talk because I could have told them something that would have made their hearts glad. I rejoice today that David and I parted forgiven.

At some point, we all come to the realization that something is terribly wrong – that some ancient code has been violated – and that violation somehow leaves us condemned – convicted of a need for forgiveness. We know that we will never be totally at ease again. That feeling – sometimes sharp and clear, sometimes dull and remote – will not leave us. I can be forgiven, but

I will never again be innocent.

Accountability has to do with loss of innocence, a loss that at first puzzles and confuses us – much like those first, early questions about the origin of babies, which are easily warded off but keep returning with greater curiosity and less satisfaction.

That initial loss of innocence leads us to ever more intense losses – to the discovery of evil and its mastery over our better intentions. Loss of innocence is always tied to an important event – at least important to the child. It could be a death, even of a pet – the birth of a brother or sister – a storm – a dream – or a physical confrontation with some moral overtones. The search for recovery, for peace, ultimately for a return to the unbounded joy of innocence, leads us ever – like the quest for the Holy Grail – back to Eden and to God.

The loss of innocence does not come once and disappear. Accountability is an ongoing process, and the pain and confusion resulting from that initial loss are only the opening pages of a book about life – a book that draws us ever more deeply into a seemingly unfathomable mystery.

My accountability began on a vacant lot, playing baseball, but it certainly did not end there. Oh, no –

and it has not ended yet.

The following stories trace a pattern of growing awareness – of increased accountability. Each event took me farther down the road of realization – each one was yet another unretraceable step toward the darkness that lostness brings.

God's providential hand was in every step. My burgeoning awareness reached an initial climax in a little restaurant in southern California, where I finally reached a depth of despair so great that only the voice and hand of God could penetrate it.

Awareness

One day, right after school, I was on the playground with some of my friends just fooling around. Mr. Dykstra, our principal, came out and began moving in our direction. It made us a little uneasy, because we didn't know him too well. I knew him better than the other kids because I was a "safety patrol."

When he got up close, he spoke to all of us at first — just general kinds of talk about school. Then he began talking just to me. He walked as he talked, and he led me away from my friends — sort of separating me from the flock, like a sheep dog does with sheep.

When we were out of hearing distance of my friends, he began to talk to me about my clothes. He pointed out that my pants were out at the knees, that there was a button missing from my shirt, and that I had a hole in one elbow. I didn't believe him at first, but when I looked, sure enough, he was right. He told me I should wear nicer clothes to school, especially since I was a safety patrol.

It bothered me.

I didn't go home in tears or anything, but it was the beginning of something. I saw that my clothes were worse than the other kids. I had never noticed it before, and it hadn't mattered. Now, I did notice it, and it did matter. In fact, it mattered very much, and every day it mattered more.

A cloud passed over my life.

The principal did me a great favor. He made me notice something I needed to notice. He wasn't harsh – in fact, he was very kind. He brought pain into my life, that's true, but it was a *growing* pain, an awareness of something about me that I needed to recognize.

Parents need to call their children's attention to things that they are ignorant of – the cutting things they say, the prejudice they express, the selfishness that motivates even some of their good deeds.

"Did you know you hurt your grandmother's feelings today?"

"Did you realize that because you were late, everyone else had to wait?"

"Did you know they were counting on you to do that?"

And most of the time, they hadn't noticed and wouldn't have cared if they had. But when parents make them aware that it matters, that awareness makes them responsible. Good parents are not unkind, cutting, or harsh, but they make their point and that creates awareness. It is that very awareness that is their children's

salvation from *selfishness*.

Selfishness

My father was a spectacularly poor manager of money. When I was about twelve, we suffered financial reverses so severe that we had to move to a *cabin* in a rather run-down trailer court. As I remember, it had four extremely small rooms. I didn't mind; in fact, I hardly noticed. My life went on about the same. I was in those last prepuberty months when life is so amazingly simple and beautiful. I played baseball till dark, roamed the neighborhood,

read comic books, ate, slept, went to school, and whistled my way through every day.

Life was good.

My sister was six years older – a senior in high school. I didn't know much about her; I knew nothing of her world, and I didn't care to find out. I would know soon enough. She was often unhappy – I knew that. We quarreled some, but never so much as we had before. She was out of my league. When we disagreed, she would just sigh and shake her head like a grownup. When she was home, she studied hard, listened to her radio, and helped with the dishes and the housework; but she never talked much, and to my twelve-year-old-mind, she was hopelessly dull. There seemed to be a certain wistfulness, or sadness, settling over her, which made her even more disagreeable to me, because I couldn't understand why anybody should be unhappy when I wasn't. There were a few times when her face showed signs of recent tears, but I had no concept of the anguish that results from humiliation and loneliness; so if I thought anything at all, I thought I must be mistaken.

At some point I began to overhear talk around the house about the senior prom. I could tell it was very important to her, but I couldn't imagine why. She needed a special dress, which we couldn't afford, and there was even some theological discussion about the propriety of her going to a dance, which perplexed me greatly. I learned that a boy from church – whom I much admired – had asked her to go. I didn't understand that either, I mean –

What did he see in my sister?

Prom night came. After supper – I couldn't help but notice that my sister didn't eat at all – we straightened up the house *again*. There was hardly anything to straighten, but I went along. She also asked me to change my clothes and to be on my best behavior, which was a bit much; but she was so earnest, so serious, that I complied with only minimal griping. She went to her bedroom to dress, and I buried myself in a comic book. My dad read the newspaper –

and time passed.

Suddenly, there was a knock at the door. My dad explained that it was Jary's date. When he came in, I thought I had never seen anybody so handsome in all my life. He looked like a prince. And then my sister came out – I simply couldn't believe it; I was dumbfounded. She had on this white formal dress, which contrasted marvelously with her long, dark hair. She was beautiful! I mean, well, she was beautiful, and I understood why he had

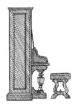

asked her. This was my sister – she lived in this house with me, we had grown up together – but I hadn't looked at her in five years, and now – there she was –

a lady.

Something about her – and him – standing there together in our living room – made me see my surroundings for the first time. Our house was shabby, pitiful, small, and mean. It smelled of rotting wood and food cooked with too much grease. It was ill-furnished with an odd assortment of tattered, scratched chairs. The couch had these covers that my mom had made to hide the stains and the worn places. It reeked of low-class poverty – which was okay for a kid like me – but not for a lady like Jary. I was embarrassed for her, and I thought,

"She deserves better than this."

I believe it was my first totally unselfish thought – a giant step on the road to maturity, but now I was troubled, because now –

I was accountable.

Puberty

This is intended as a tribute to all of those who have taught junior high. Teaching junior high school for seven years led me to two inescapable conclusions – well, actually three. First, when junior high teachers die, they go straight to heaven – there is no standing in line, no question-and-answer period, and no looking in record books; they don't go to paradise first, either. When a junior high teacher shows up at the pearly gates, Saint Peter says, "You look like a junior high teacher."

"How did you know that?"

"Oh, by your age, first – junior high teachers get here younger than most others. Second, by the look of relief on your face when you woke up and discovered you were dead and didn't even know if you were going to heaven or hell. And third, by the way you looked around frantically to see if any of your students were here."

"Well, you're right, I am a junior high teacher. Just promise me that I won't have to teach junior high any more, and I won't care where you send me."

"Michael, send this one

straight to the gold room."

It's that simple. No amount of bad living or bad ideas will keep a junior high teacher from the pearly gates. It's a better guarantee than martyrdom – I mean, like being burned at the stake – although it's very similar.

My second conclusion is that it is a big mistake to take junior high students seriously in the area of academics. It is a great waste of time and money to try to teach junior high kids anything – you see, their brains are not in a *learning* mode. When puberty sets in, a biological phenomenon takes place, and a kid's brain gets coated with a symbiotic fluid that causes it to float in a sort of nebulous position. This is what produces that characteristic vacant stare on junior high students' faces every time they are asked a question. On the first day of school, the kids wander into your classroom like they've never seen one before. You hear them say things like, "Hey, what's that?"

"Uh, what?"

"That thing over there."

"Uh, I don't know. What you do you think it is?"

"I think it's what they called a *girl* last year – in fact, I'm almost sure."

They sit down, after the fight over who gets the last seat in the back row, and you look at those blank faces and think, "This is going to be a *very* long year. Why me? Why do I do this to myself?"

So you try to develop a little rapport with them. You pick out the most intelligent face you can find – which is not easy – and you say, "What's your name, son?"

The kid sits and stares at you. You think maybe you picked the wrong one, but then again, maybe he has a hearing deficiency; so you move over, right in front of him, and you look deep into those glassy eyes, and you slowly repeat the question, "What's – your – name – son?"

The kid looks wildly around the room – finally, he puts his finger to his chest and says – "You mean me?"

"Yes, I mean *you.*" You say it very gently so as not to disturb his train of thought, or whatever you call what is going on in his brain – I mean, between his ears.

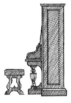

Coming
of Age

♦

98

"What – is – your – name?" You repeat the question, because you know he's forgotten it by now.

"Uh – you mean you want to know *my* name?"

"Yes! Yes! That's exactly what I mean." And you're really excited. Maybe this won't be such a bad year after all; this kid is catching on really fast.

"Well, uh, don't push me. I'm not too good under pressure. I know the answer to this one." His face contorts with the effort, and then a light comes on. "It's Frank! Yeah, it's Frank!" You've never seen such happiness. "I got it right, didn't I?" And he looks at the kid next to him for confirmation. "I got it right on the very first try!" and he looks proudly at his classmates.

"That's great, Frank; now let's go for the big one. What's your last name?"

Your heart is pounding, because you know that you may have reached too far, too soon. The kid sits and stares – looks around the room again, and finally comes back to your penetrating look.

"You mean me, *again?* Why don't you pick on someone else – I can't be expected to carry the load for the whole class, you know."

Sometimes, in severe cases, these kids' brains go into reverse, but most of the time they get stuck in one groove – *reproduction*. I mean, like sexual reproduction – in case junior high has been so long ago for you that you have forgotten the relationship between those words. You can teach them anything that has to do with *reproduction*. If you say that King George and Queen Ann tried hard to produce an heir to the throne for many years without success, so George produced a child by another lady who became George the III, suddenly they will be transfixed. Their ears will be tuned to every word, and history will be transformed into something exciting, relevant, and wonderful. You science teachers need to stop talking about monoecious and dioecious and start talking about how two swinging conifers decide to get together to make a little conifer. I tell you that those dull, bored, blank, lifeless eyes will turn into agitated pools of eager anticipation. If you English teachers say that there is an erotic relationship between a subject and a verb that means they simply cannot get along without each other, little beads of perspiration will form on the boys' upper lips, and the girls will giggle. Any subject that is related to reproduction will create a learning sensation –

if it's not about reproduction,
you can forget it.

My third conclusion is that I should qualify for permanent disability on the basis of my mental condition after seven years of teaching junior high. This is the time of "Tru Luv 4 ever" – for the seventh time in three weeks – and "Best Friends" – until I find someone else.

It can't be avoided – it has to happen. It's the price parents and teachers pay for the sins of their youth. The only consolation I have for you is that it passes – it takes about four years, actual time, and about twenty years off your life expectancy – but it passes.

I especially want to honor junior high *English* teachers, because they have to teach *poetry*. This is the most excruciatingly painful experience imaginable. Not only do they have to teach it and watch those silly grins as those pubescent little minds pick up every possible sexual innuendo, write it down, and pass it to the kid next to them – junior high teachers have to assign the writing of poetry, and then they have to read the doggerel that is turned in. Some of it isn't too bad – unless they try to get serious, or worse yet, try to copy the style and language of some of the people they study. Here's a sampling of some that are tolerable.

> "My dog's dead
> Cause he got fits.
> I dropped Larry
> Cause he got zits."

You can even appreciate the ingenuity of stuff like –

> "Thirty days have Septober,
> April, June, and no wonder.
> All the rest have peanut butter
> Except my grandmother,
> She rides a little red tricycle."

Or better yet –

> "One day when I entered the John,
> I spied Jimmy sitting upon
> a white marble throne,
> he was there all alone.
>
> He sat straight up on the stool.
> He cried 'Stephanie called me a fool.'
> I still can't believe – bless my soul,
> He jumped up and dove down the hole.
>
> His mind was in such a state,
> I hurried to help – but too late.
> I blew it; I knew I should rush it.
> I guessed he was gone – so I flushed it."

Martha, Martha

It was her eighth-grade year, and she was painfully aware of herself – her body, her hair, even the way she walked and talked. Her face was clear, with a sprinkling of freckles; her eyes were deep set and sensitive; she had soft, full lips; and her nose wrinkled when she laughed. She had an "unspoiled" look – she looked like God had just created her yesterday. She was on the thin side – *gangly* would perhaps be an apt description. Her legs and arms were long, and there were indications of a coming grace. But her facial and physical features did not result in that special structure of bone and flesh that we call beauty.

No. She was decidedly not pretty.

I had first met her as a seventh grader in my English class and then as a soprano in the junior high choir, which I directed. We had developed a relationship – she was a decent, level-headed, respectful kid – and we were friends; we liked each other. Because I had taught several years at this level, I knew most of the social goings on. I knew there was a certain boy she wished would "notice" her. We talked about it a little, but it was an almost sacred subject with her, and she tried to deny it – even with me – if I hinted too strongly at such an interest.

Unfortunately, she had set her affections on a boy, who in my opinion, was totally unworthy of her, one who I knew hadn't the slightest interest in a girl who was quiet and totally lacking in the type of "glitter appeal" that characterizes the junior high jet set. He was one of those boys who achieves full physical maturity at fourteen. He had broad shoulders, dark, curly hair, a dark complexion, white, even teeth, and a dazzling smile. Streetwise, cocky, reasonably intelligent – in a sort of animalistic way – and fully cognizant of his charms, he was the epitome of the junior high idol – the kind of face that appeared on the posters pasted inside

every girl's locker.

I discovered that she was convinced she could attract him if only she were allowed to wear makeup – but her parents did not allow her to wear it, and so she blamed them for her social problems. She was wrong – it wouldn't have mattered – but I couldn't convince her. I understood her problem – I understood then, and I understand now. It is a predestined thing, ordained in the Garden of Eden and integrated into man's emotional circuitry. "You must at some time in your life break your heart over the unattainable, the inaccessible, and yes – the unworthy.

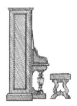

Only then can you become a complete person."

One day in late spring, I was on lunch-hour playground duty, standing by one of the buildings, surrounded by a chaotic mob of laughing, teasing, milling juveniles. I noticed her standing alone outside the circle. She cast a sideways glance at me that meant she wanted to talk, so I began moving and sending the others away. When they were finally gone, she approached – slowly, head down, shoes scuffing the sand. I could see that she was distraught. When she got close enough, she threw her arms around me, buried her face in my chest, and sobbed out the story. She had finally summoned the courage to write a note to him. Not only had he made a joke out of it, he had showed the note to all of his friends – everyone in school had seen it and had been teasing her. Junior high kids can be brutal –

totally without compassion.

When she finally gained control, she looked up – straight into my eyes – and said, "Mr. Smith, am I pretty?"

At that moment – with her eyelashes still wet from the tears, with the fierce agony in her eyes, with her cheeks flushed with emotion, I could have honestly said, "Yes," but that was not the question –

and that was not the answer.

What an infinity of longing lay behind her question. In our culture, it is one of the ultimate inquiries. I didn't know what to say. My answer was important to her. She trusted me, so I had to be truthful. I knew that I mustn't throw out some meaningless tripe – some evasive jargon that would sidestep the question and give hope where there was none.

"No, Jeanine, you're not pretty – at least not yet and not as you mean it. But we need to talk about it. I have something to share with you that is more important than being pretty; although I know that's very important to you right now."

We walked to the chorus room, which I knew was empty, and into my office there. I let her cry for a while and encouraged her to talk about her feelings. I knew I needed to assure her of my love and that I accepted and understood the reality of her pain. I also knew that I needed to shift her focus away from herself and the present situation. First, I shared with her a story from my own junior high experience (the next story in this section), and then I took out a New Testament that I kept there and read the following passage: "Martha, Martha, you are worried and bothered about so many things, but only one is necessary. For Mary has chosen what is best, and it will not be taken away from her."

Yes, I shared this passage with this fourteen-year-old girl, and even at her age, I think she understood the compassion and sympathy of our Lord and what he was trying to say about

important things.

I wonder where she is now – that young lady, now grown – probably with children of her own. I wonder if she remembers that time and if she shares it with her little girls. I wonder what kind of mother she is, and I wonder if she is still worried about being pretty. I wonder if she has gained a greater understanding of the One who

shared His life with us.

Dragons and Princesses

How should we be able to forget those ancient myths that are at the beginning of all peoples, the myths about dragons that at the last moment turn into princesses; perhaps all the dragons of our lives are princesses who are only waiting to see us, once beautiful and brave. Perhaps everything terrible is in its deepest being something helpless that wants help from us.

—Rainer Maria Rilke, *Letters to a Young Poet*

Alec Redmon lived on Rochester Road, about a half mile from me. I had to pass his house on my way to school and on my way home. Alec was a bully. He had been held back in school and he was older, taller, and stronger than the rest of us. He had threatened me, shoved me around, knocked my books out of my hands, and knocked my hat off. He had baited and provoked me in every conceivable way – taunting and heckling and knowing that I dared not challenge his vastly superior size and strength. I was terrified of him. What he did to me physically was absolutely nothing compared to the mental anguish – the anxiety produced by my imagination every morning and afternoon.

In order to avoid him, I went blocks out of my way, taking long detours, and varying my route so he would never know exactly which way I had gone. But one afternoon, I forgot about Alec. I was so preoccupied with whatever thought I was pursuing, that I did not take any of my detours. I was not aware of my mistake until I was shaken from my reverie by the sound of Alec's voice

calling my name.

I stopped dead in my tracks, my heart beating wildly, my mind racing, my mouth suddenly dry, and with a nauseating sickness in my stomach. He ran across the road – right up to me – and I prepared for the worst.

He said, "Hey, John, we got that big test in history tomorrow, and you're pretty good in there – would you come over tonight and help me study?"

I was stunned, absolutely speechless – the thought of Alec needing my help with anything was beyond my comprehension. Alec, obviously thinking that I would refuse, began to apologize for all of his meanness – he paused, looking down, and he said quietly, "I'm really sorry for all the mean things I've done to you. I don't know why I do them, and sometimes, afterward, I hate myself. John, I really need some help; if I fail that test, I'm going to be held back again."

"I guess I could do that," I mumbled.

"Thanks, John; it would mean a lot to me. Thanks a lot."

I went home very thoughtfully, not at all sure I had done the right thing. When I asked my mother for permission to go to Alec's house, she said, "Isn't that the boy you've had so much trouble with?"

"Yes, ma'am."

"Do you think it's wise to go over there?"

I told my mother what had happened that afternoon, and she told me that I was doing exactly what Jesus would do. That made me feel better, but you need to know that my walk to the Redmon's house that night was one of the most daring and brave things I have ever done. Many things in my later life, which might appear to have required courage, pale into insignificance in comparison to what it took to keep going that night.

The Redmon's had their porch light on, and Mrs. Redmon met me at the door. *I had never thought of Alec Redmon having a mother* – it seemed incongruous. Somehow the fact that he had one was reassuring. She was a

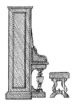

very nice lady, and she thanked me over and over for coming to help Alec. The Redmon house was much larger than ours, but it smelled about the same. All houses and families have a smell, you know – that's how dogs know their owners – it's just that you get so used to your own smell that you don't notice it, but you sure notice other people's smells because they're different. The Redmon's house smelled different, but not much, and

it wasn't a bad difference.

Alec and I went up to his room to study. I could tell you a lot about his room – but it's enough to say that it was pretty much like mine.

What I found out, studying with Alec, was that *he couldn't read.* I couldn't believe it – I mean reading was the easiest thing in the world, and it was fun too – and *Alec couldn't read* – not even the simple stuff. As I read to him and explained what the words meant and tried to help him understand about the Civil War and how it affected our country, something happened. It was not a conscious thought, but somehow, even then, I knew I would never, ever be afraid of Alec Redmon again – how could I be afraid of someone who couldn't read? I felt sorry for Alec.

Imagine that – me feeling sorry for Alec.

I could add that Alec and I became friends – pretty good friends – and remained friends until I moved away.

I ask you to read again the words at the beginning of this story. I only pause to add that the world is full of dragons – Alec Redmons – we are confronted with them at every turn. It is the mission of every Christian to learn and to show how Jesus converts dragons into princesses – not just by changing *them,* but by opening our eyes

and changing *us.*

I also need to say that my faith in goodness has been restored. Oh, it has been refined and expanded, but it is much the same now as it was when I was a child.

Goodness *will prevail.* Make no mistake about it. There is an absolute power and safety in goodness that evil cannot overcome. How could we possibly be disciples of Jesus and not believe that. Jesus said that the meek would inherit the earth. The triumph of goodness is assured by God himself because he is good, and just as surely as God lives, so goodness lives.

Do not be afraid to align yourself with goodness.
The victories of evil are short-lived
and self-destructive.

Goodness will prevail.

Billy's Team

Billy Hicks was the epitome of all the idols ever imagined by a junior high boy. He was everything the rest of us wanted to be. He was a head taller than us; he was muscular, amazingly fast on his feet, agile — by far the best athlete in school — and so strong that no one ever thought of challenging him. In addition, he was very good looking. He had beautiful, blond hair that curled all over his head, and his complexion was absolutely flawless — no traces of acne or chicken pox scars anywhere. His features were sharply defined — he might have modeled for a sculpture of a Greek god.

He had one other attribute that needs mentioning. You might think that these qualities would have made him arrogant, vain, or most likely, a bully. He wasn't. Billy was as mild mannered, as easy going, as good natured as a Saint Bernard pup.

And when it came to girls — Billy had a way with them. They flocked around him, pleading for just a little of his attention, and Billy gave it to them — all of them — it didn't matter if they were pretty or not. He was so at ease — laughing, teasing, complimenting, and making every one of them think she was special —

he amazed me.

If he had a flaw, it was that he was a very poor student. Somewhere along the course of his educational career, he had been held back, and I never ceased to be amazed at his lack of knowledge about history or his inability to fathom the simplest concepts in math. He had no notion where Central America was or what Congress was, and nouns and verbs were a mystery to him. His academic failures did nothing to diminish him in our eyes. We covered for him and constantly came to his aid, but it never bothered Billy not to know.

Even the teachers loved Billy.

Although I loved Billy, idolized him, tagged along behind him everywhere, and basked in the sunlight of those who seemed to occupy a special place in his "inner circle," I was frustrated by him. Those junior high years are so critical. I was so sensitive, so aware of myself — trying to figure out who I was and beginning to notice girls for the first time. Until then, I had never understood why God had even made girls – they were the silliest and most useless things in creation – except my mother, of course – but then she wasn't a girl. But I could never think of anything to say to a girl – and now I wanted badly to say something, but I would just stand there, hands in pockets, head down –

embarrassed and speechless.

I was also trying to establish myself as a budding athlete – to find my own place in the arena. All of the questions, the frustrations, the bewildering incomprehensibilities – they were all present in me, all at once – and Billy – well, Billy somehow stood squarely between me and the answers.

We attended a large junior high in Royal Oak, Michigan. There was only one other junior high in the area; so we played intramural sports. The teams were poorly supervised, and for the most part, were left to the discretion of the boys. Everybody wanted to be on Billy's team. There were only two teams, actually – Billy's team – and the "other team." Since I was the second or third best athlete, I could never be on Billy's team. I had to select the "other team"; it was never "my team" or "John's team," just –

the "other team."

When we picked teams, the boys would beg me not to select them. They would try to hide behind each other when it was my turn to pick. If I did select them, they hated me because nobody could beat Billy's team. No matter what sport we played, Billy simply could not lose – it was unthinkable. Even if I had the best all-around team – which often happened because Billy didn't care much who he picked – we would still lose. Take a boy who was minimally talented, place him on Billy's team, and he would hit home runs, make spectacular pass receptions in football, and sink long jump shots in basketball. Boys who were normally good athletes – on the "other team" – could do nothing right.

Billy made the difference.

And I wanted to win – I needed to win – it was an obsession with me. Only God knows how hard I tried to beat Billy. My heart ached with it. I lay awake at night, scheming of ways to win and dreaming of what it would be like to win – just once. I broke my heart trying to win.

It couldn't be done.

I also wanted to be on Billy's team. I honestly would have given much to be less talented so I could stand among the throng and plead to be picked when it was Billy's turn, because winning meant to be on Billy's team. But it could not be – the pattern was set – I must always stand on the other side and pick the losing team.

My eighth-grade year passed slowly, painfully, and we moved on to high school. Eventually, Billy passed out of my life. He dropped out of school his sophomore year, when his bountiful good nature and warm personality were no longer sufficient to pass his subjects. I never saw him again, and

I have often wondered what became of him.

There are three ideas that come to me from that time. The first is how desperately parents need to be sensitive to their junior high children and understanding toward the pain, frustration, and bewilderment that lies behind the masked faces that come home from school – those faces that, when asked how things went at school, always avert themselves from the questioner and say, "Oh, fine." I never talked to my parents about girls or about Billy. They didn't know that he existed. I didn't know how to do it, and I had no hope that they would understand. I'm sure they often wondered what was wrong when I came home from school – went straight to my room – and did not appear again until called for supper. I wanted to talk about it – I needed to talk about it – but my parents never shared their experiences from those years,

so I bore my pain alone.

The second idea is that *Billy made the difference* – he really did. Just knowing they were on Billy's team transformed those weak and mediocre boys. Not only did they perform well – they were willing to reach out – to try what they would never have tried without him. Oh, how parents need to provide an incentive to their children by showing them that Jesus makes the difference in our lives. Knowing Jesus – and being on His team – can and will transform us. Not only can we perform far beyond our expectations, we can reach for new horizons both spiritually and physically – knowing that on His team we cannot fail.

We can lose –
but we cannot fail.

The third idea is that even as adults we want to "win." Share with your children that your heart still aches with it. We all want to win in life – to feel that we matter – that our lives have value and purpose. But show them that beyond that, you have another longing that runs far deeper – a longing to be wanted and to belong. As children of God, born again into his family, we have the thrill of victory – a victory of such far-reaching consequences that all incidental losses are swallowed up. God has chosen us to be on His team – and that's even better than being on –

Billy's team.

The Value of Suffering

It was very late – actually early in the morning – but long before dawn, when I heard the phone ring. He answered. I heard him talking earnestly, but quietly, and I eventually went back to sleep. Some time later I was awakened by his voice. He was at my door, his body framed by the light in the hallway, and he was calling to me, "Dad? Dad?"

"Yes," I said.

"I hate to wake you up, but I need to talk to you."

He came and sat on the edge of my bed, but he could not speak. His entire body was racked with such devastation that he trembled. I rolled over and sat beside him, putting my arms around him and pressing him to me like I had when he was a child.

He did not want to cry, he fought it with every ounce of strength he had. He was, he thought, too old to cry, too accomplished, too educated and sophisticated. His body convulsed with the struggle; he tried to speak – and then he cried. It was like the sudden breaking of a dam. He cried because life had been cruel and had delivered a crushing blow at a most inopportune moment. He said he had fallen in love – he had, but she had not.

He cried because
he was only a boy –
a boy who was trying
to become a man.

We sat on the edge of the bed, and he tried to tell me how much he hurt – how sick he was – he felt like throwing up. I understood. I had been sick, too, and I told him about that. But I don't think he heard me. And if he did, he could not relate *my experience* in the context of *his grief*, because he thought – like all of us did that first time – that his grief was somehow different from all others.

Because I thought he was old enough, I talked to him of suffering and its redemptive value. I told him that suffering and grieving were *great gifts* – giant steps in the process of *knowing God*. I cautioned him that grieving for personal loss was a necessary step toward learning to grieve with others.

Self-centered suffering is necessary – it must always come first – but it can become self-serving if it does not lead us to suffer for others – to understand their heartaches and pains.

I also tried to tell him that when he had learned to suffer for others, his own sufferings would diminish – not because they were less or fewer, but because he would not take them into account. I even tried to share with him what I had learned from the Bible and David's grief over his rebellious son, Absolom. Dostoevsky had phrased it best for me in *The Brothers Karamazov* –

"God, help me to be *worthy* of my sufferings."

That is an idea worth reaching for.

I told him that this would pass – though he did not believe me – that time would leave only a small scar to remind him of the step he had taken. I told him I hoped that he would somehow know that he was a better man in his grief than he had ever been in his joy – that he was far closer to the springs of life, the essence of fleshly experience here, than he would ever be anywhere else – that he was closer to the heart of love, of God Himself, than he had ever been before.

He said that he needed to go to her – that he needed to see her face – and look into her eyes when she said the words. She was a thousand miles away. I tried at first to dissuade him, telling him how foolish it was – that he needed to accept it and go on with his life. But then I remembered – I remembered another time and another girl, and I told him to go – to go quickly, immediately – not to rest until he had satisfied his need. I helped him pack and he left.

It was still dark.

Thirty-six hours later, he was back. He had not slept. (It's wonderful to be young and in love.) He had seen her – they had talked. Nothing was changed – nothing except my son – he was changed. He would never be the same –

awareness was upon him.

The years have passed, and my son is now a man. He is happily married, and he has a son of his own, and another on the way. Much has happened to both of us since that night, but he has never forgotten. I felt then that our talk had made little impact or impression – time has proved me wrong. I praise God for that time and for the bond that was made that night.

My son has proved to be
worthy of his suffering

She's All Right

It nearly always comes at night, and most of the time it's very late. I had been asleep for some time when the phone rang. I fumbled clumsily in the dark for the receiver, knocking the Kleenex box onto the floor – then tipping the lamp over. Muttering under my breath that if this was a wrong number or a solicitation of some sort – somebody was going to get an earful. I finally found the phone and mumbled the kind of "Hello" that means this had better be important. The only sound was that uninterrupted, pregnant silence that creates apprehension and then this word – "Dad!" Just the one word – and then silence again.

I was fully awake.

"Yes!"

"Dad!"

"Kris? – What's wrong?"

The next sound I heard is known to every parent – every person. From the cradle to the grave – it is the universal cure for heartbreak. She had held it as long as she could – long enough to make a call – because there is only one thing worse than grieving – and that is

grieving alone.

Her pain was so intense that she could not speak – and all I could do was listen – and grieve with her – and dread. The list of potential explanations was not comforting – disease, drugs, pregnancy, failing grades, dismissal from school, death or injury to someone close to us. You don't want to believe any of those things – everybody knows that in real life they only happen to other people's kids – but it doesn't stop you from imagining them. The sobbing subsided, temporarily, and the story began to come out. Haltingly, she told me that she had broken up with her boyfriend – not just a boyfriend, but a boy she had given her heart to and hoped to marry – a boy she loved. She was devastated – I was relieved. No, I really was. I'm not proud of it – and I know it's a little brutal and even self-serving – but that was the first thing I felt – relief.

"Thank God," I thought.
"It's *only* that."

She vented her *frustration* — because she didn't understand; her *anger* — because she felt betrayed; her *loneliness and isolation* — because it was her first time and because she thought she was the only one. As she talked, I realized what distance means — we were so far apart — and I also realized how helpless I was to touch her pain.

I couldn't fix this one.

"Can I come home?" she said. "Dad, I just want to be in my own room and sleep in my own bed. Please — let me come home."

"Oh, my dearest child," I thought, "how I know what you're feeling — how I understand how a broken heart turns toward home — what a compliment to your mother and I that in the hour of your greatest need, you have remembered home and turned to us. You need healing — and the balm of home is the only healing you know. But, my dearest, the world will not go away, and not even home can provide the medication you need."

"Of course," I said. "Mom and I would love to see you."

But even as I said it, I was aware of how much I *wanted* her to come home — how badly I *wanted* to provide the answers — to fix this, to soothe and smooth and approve her. I wanted her to depend on *me* — to find her center in us — and even then, I knew that what *I* wanted — needed — was not what *she* needed. I knew that if she didn't deal with this on her own — if she came home *now* — she would come home again.

"What would you do here, honey? You have no friends here — nothing to occupy your time. Mom and I would have to work — what would you do all day?"

"I don't know, Dad, I just don't know what to do."

"I don't know, either, but it seems to me that you would be very lonesome — and eventually, *you'll have to go back.* Wouldn't it be easier to face it now? You do know you will have to go back — don't you?"

"I hadn't thought about that," she said, as though it was just now occurring to her that her world was the only one that had crashed and that even a crashed world would not prevent tomorrow. We talked on and on — and even as we talked — she grew up a little.

"I guess there's no more coming home for me, is there, Dad?" It was an aching question and I ached in reply, but I was glad that *she* had asked it.

"No, Kris, there's no more coming home."

"Oh, my love," I thought, "my baby, my darling girl — all things are struck real for you in this moment — it is a cruel world after all. Now we both know

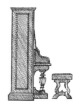

Coming
of Age

◆

111

that you are beyond my healing – that even home, familiar walls, your own bed, and our love are not enough to replace the emptiness that is in your heart."

"Dad, will you and Mom pray for me?"

"Of course; we always do."

"But, would you especially pray for me right now. It's the only hope I have."

"Yes," I thought, "it is the only hope we have ever had, but it takes times like these to realize it. You will forget – but the next time your heart breaks, you will remember more easily, and you will turn in the direction of Him who also wept – and some day – when Mom and I are gone – He will truly be your only hope and refuge."

"I'll be all right now, Dad," she said confidently. "Don't worry."

"Yes, you will be all right," I said, and I thought, "You'll be all right – until you hang up and try to go to sleep, and then it will all come back fresh upon you – but finally, you will be all right. Of course, that won't keep us from worrying – it's never that easy."

"I love you, Dad – more than ever."

"I love you too." They weren't exactly the same things – her love and mine – but they were closer than they had ever been – much closer. I hadn't moved much – but she had made a quantum leap.

I hung up, and my wife – who was wide awake – said, "Is she all right?" It's tough – hearing half a conversation.

"Yes, honey, she's all right. In fact, she's more all right than she's been in some time, but the next few days are going to be tough on her."

"Is she coming home?"

"No, she's not coming home – we've lost our baby. She's becoming – what we raised her to be. She's all right."

I wouldn't want to do it again –
raise my kids I mean,
but doing it has created a wonder –
an understanding
and a sense of dependence on God
that I would never have had
without it.

He Is There

It was the low point of my young life. I was in my early twenties. I had been preaching for five or six years. I was unmarried – not by choice but by *providence*. A combination of finding myself at odds with church leaders over some longstanding understandings of Scripture – unable to harmonize the realities of life with the unreality of many church traditions – the growing awareness of the reality of sin in my own life, not so much *overt* sin, as much as the depth of evil that I was capable of conceiving – my inability to deal with that sin or find cleansing – and the loss of a relationship with a girl I had hoped to marry – all of this left me terribly depressed, lonely, and emotionally disturbed.

In an effort to regain my balance, I left home – I left all that was familiar to me and hitchhiked from Michigan to Los Angeles, California. I had no specific destination or plan in mind. Los Angeles was the farthest place I knew – a place I had never been. I wanted to see the ocean, and most of the rides I got were headed in that general direction.

After much shifting around – sleeping on park benches – on beaches and in Salvation Army centers, I found myself employed as a clean-up man at a mobile home factory in Lomita, California. I took a room at the Lomita Hotel – a shabby, run-down, disreputable establishment – which was home to several longshoremen. I took a room there because it was cheap, because they would wait till I got paid for their rent, and because it was close enough to my work for me to walk.

I was friendless and broke.

I sold two or three articles of clothing for food money, but it didn't last. I found myself with four days to go until payday and no money. I did okay the first day, but it was hot at work, and my job entailed swinging an eight-pound sledge hammer for hours at a time. It depleted my physical reserves in a hurry. After the second day, I was a little weak and even a little dizzy. The third day I was barely able to walk back to the hotel. I was desperate. I borrowed a dollar from one of the longshoremen, and that night I went to the owner-operated diner just down the street and sat on a stool at the counter.

Even in those days, a dollar didn't buy much. I went over the menu slowly, meticulously, trying to get the most for my dollar. I ordered a *pork dinner*, and when it came, I tried to eat slowly –

savoring each bite.

While I was eating, I began to think about my mother's cooking – and I thought about Michigan and home – I thought about church potlucks, gospel singings, my friends, and what I used to be. The full realization of my lostness, hopelessness, and sinfulness settled over me. I saw clearly how far I had fallen and what I had become. A blanket of black depression, regret, and guilt settled over me – such as I had never experienced. I rested my head on my arms, which were on the counter, and I wept.

I scarcely noticed that a man had come in and occupied the stool next to me. I became aware of him when he turned and tried to console me in an almost unintelligible way. He was obviously very drunk. He had ordered the largest steak dinner on the menu, and it was served to him just as I raised my head. He looked at it – shoved it across the counter – stated emphatically that he didn't want it –

paid for it – and left.

The owner-cook must have sensed my desperate condition as I stared unbelievingly at the forsaken plate. "You want this, buddy?" he asked.

It was delicious! In some ways, a small gesture. But to a lost and wandering child – to a person at the end of his rope, a person who was seeking a place to stand, a reason to be – it was a ray of hope. It was a friendly hand on my shoulder, a reassuring voice calling my name out of the darkness. "John – son – I'm still here. Don't lose heart. I'm watching – I'm concerned – I'll see you through this."

I want you to see that only because of the condition I was in was I able to see the hand of God. Under ordinary conditions, I would have tossed it off as circumstantial; I would have said, "Now, wasn't that weird?" But God wasn't through with me – no – He wasn't through at all. In fact, He was just getting me ready for the next step. When I got back to the hotel, filled with gratitude and the absolute wonder of what had just happened, the lady at the front desk told me she had a letter for me.

It was from my mother.

Read this letter, parents – consider the circumstances under which I received it – and never question the value of your role or the *providence* that brings you precious opportunities.

A Letter from Home

The following letter from my mother was waiting when I returned to the hotel after eating. It appears here as close to its original form as possible and practical. I have spelled the words as she spelled them, and I have placed in italics what she had underlined. One page in her original hand is included as well. My mother had only an elementary school education. Some explanations will be helpful.

"Hoy" is my brother-in-law, who is also a preacher.

"Birmingham" is Birmingham, Michigan, close to where I grew up. My parents were "charter members" there.

"Susie Q's" is a fish and chips restaurant on Woodward Avenue, just north of Ten Mile Road in Royal Oak, Michigan.

"Sister Clyde Utley" was the wife of Brother L. C. Utley, to whom I am deeply indebted. He was the preacher for at least two of the churches I attended as a boy. He was the first person to get me up front to lead singing and to answer Bible questions. He was the most kind, patient, loving, soft-spoken preacher I ever knew.

"Mary Crosslin" was the wife of Earl Crosslin, and they were dear friends of my family at the Rochester Church of Christ in Rochester, Michigan, where Michigan Christian College is now located.

My mother says – concerning the Bible she had received – that it was a "King James of course." This is because we had a longstanding feud in our house about *versions.* My brother-in-law Hoy and I had both switched to the American Standard, which my mother considered scandalous. She would never read anything but the King James, which she felt had been used by the apostle Paul on Mars Hill. Hoy and I referred to her Bible as the "King James *Vision,"* which did not help resolve the argument.

I tell you these things to help you understand how each name made an impact on me by stirring my memories of that happy time. I also know that every sensitive reader will learn much about the type of person my mother was.

Friday, Jan. 19, 1962
(Date your letters)

Dear Son,

Well, we just received your letter (wish you would date your letters so I would know just when you wrote.)

Hope you are feeling lots better and working real hard. God has said to, "Be content with such things as you have, for, He has said, I will never leave you, nor forsake you." What a consolation. This ought to comfort you, Son. I know God will take care of you and He will bless you according to, *His Will*. Love Him and trust Him and believe in Him. He will see you through all your trials. I pray for you, Son, every morning when I am driving to work. When I am working. When I drive home at night. When I go to bed. When I wake up in the morning. I *know God* is with you, and I trust in Him to take care of you. I'm too far away from you, but God is everywhere. He knows where you are, what you are, and every move you make, so I pray to Him for you. May you get well, and be again a minister of the Gospel.

I must go to work so will write more when I have time.

Well, my day's work is done and I'm back home. Boy, it's cold here and snowing again. I'd like to finish this letter pretty quick and go to bed and keep warm under three blankets. Say, how are your clothes? Do you need more? How do you get them clean?

I'm glad to hear you have started working. Although I do not care for you in that kind of environment, but as long as God is with you, all things will work out o.k., I know. Try hard to make the best of it, honey, and try to get a preaching job again. This would please God, and me too. Can't you wear work gloves in what you are working at?

Now, you asked me to read James 5:13–18 and I have just read it. Elias must have been a righteous man because the 16th verse says "The effectual fervent prayer of a righteous man availeth much." Now my question is how *righteous* are you? Examine yourself. You should know the answer. You did a lot of good for the Lord when you were going about preaching the Word, comforting the sick, converting the sinners, but now you have left your first love, you have *quit working* for the Lord, and instead have fallen in love in a worldly manner. Falling in love with a girl you would want to marry is alright, son, but to forsake the Lord's work is a sin. No man putting his hands to the plow and looking back is fit for the kingdom of Heaven. God has given you a talent. You worked with it for a while, but now you have buried it. Do you expect God to give you what you ask for when you have forsaken

Dear Son: (Date your letters) Friday 19, 1962

Well, we just received your letter (wish you would date your) letters so I would know just when you wrote.

Hope you are feeling lots better and working real hard. God has said to "Be content with such things as you have, for He has said, I will never leave you nor forsake you." What a consolation. This ought to comfort you, Son, I know God will take care of you, and He will bless you according to, His Will. Love Him and Trust Him and believe in Him. He will see you through all your trials. I Pray for you, Son, every morning when I am driving to work. When I am working. When I drive home

His commandments to go, preach the Gospel? These are straight forward questions, Son, but I hope they will help you see the light.

I just finished reading Ps. 27:1–14. Yes, Son, wait on the Lord. Be of good courage wait, wait on the Lord and He will give you strength. Read Ps. 28:7, and apply it to yourself. Ps. 34:17, 18, 19. These verses should give you strength. The 16th verse tells us that if we are evil the Lord will turn His face from us. The 18th verse gives you hope that God will be with you. The 19th verse the *righteous* have afflictions and *many*, but the Lord is there to deliver him *out of them* all. So Son, believe that the Lord will do this (if you are righteous).

Oh! I must go to bed it's 10:30 p.m. See you tomorrow (Lord willing).

Good morning. It's 7:50 a.m. Dad has left for work and I am back on the davenport where I slept all night. We had pancakes and sausage for breakfast. The Birmingham Church is having a fellowship dinner tonight at the YMCA building in Birmingham. I am to take chicken and dressing, sure wish you could come too. I'm a little bit afraid of you being in such a ruff place, Son, but I keep telling myself that God will take care of you never mind where you are.

Son, until this thing happened to you, you were such a *good* sound *preacher* of the *Gospel* and a *wonderful teacher* and *song leader*. God gave you all these talents so you could use them in His service. Don't you know and realize that if you would pick up where you left off, and continue working with these talents in His service God will be more apt to answer your fervent prayers to Him.

You know the Bible well. It's up to you as a child of God to *go out* and *preach it*. God is holding you responsible. The Scriptures tell Christians to *reprove, rebuke,* and *exhort* with *all* long *suffering,* and doctrine, and this is what I am *trying* to do for you, Son. Please think on these things.

Hoy, gave me a new Bible last Sunday (a King James of course) and it's so very nice. I think this is the fourth or fifth one I've had since becoming a member of God's Family. I've got them all saved and put away.

Son, you *must believe* and trust God in *every one* of the Scriptures. Why do you question some of the scriptures. You say, "I believe or am at least *trying* too." Every scripture is given to us by God and without *faith* it's *impossible* to believe in him. Why, Son, I *believe every word* that *God* has *written* in the *scriptures.* Do you believe me? You have known the Holy Scriptures from your youth, up. When you *couldn't read or write* I taught them to you. If I didn't believe in them would I have taken my time to teach them to you? I wish I could shrink you up to where you would be about two years old so I could start all over again to bring you up, knowing what I know now. I know that

Coming
of Age

◆

118

could never be so I must try my very best to convince you of where you have done wrong and are still doing wrong by forsaking the Lord's work.

Sunday night, 7:30, Dad is in bed snoring away and I'm on the davenport again, all ready for bed, just wanted to finish this letter so I can get it mailed early in the morning.

We didn't go to church tonight, Dad had a very bad headache and the weather is sort of freezing rain. We had dinner with the Moody's after church today. Went to Susie Q's. Then we all went to a singing at Rochester. Mary Crosslin asked me to say "Hello" to you for her and that she is praying for you. Sister Clyde Utley said the same thing. Every where we go some one or more ask us how you are. There are so many of your brethren that are very much concerned about you. I tell them you are making out o.k., or something to that effect. I hope, I'm not wrong in telling them this much about you. I would love to tell all who ask me how very well you are doing and feeling real proud of such a wonderful son. I pray God that He will give you strength and help you through this terrible ordeal that has such a bearing on you, and keeping you so tied up in a knot.

Honey, I want you to try real hard to get along on your own. I have faith in you and all the confidence in the world that you can make it by yourself.

Well, Sweetie, I've enjoyed writing this letter to you although it's taken me three days off and on but I'm about to sign off.

I sent my first letter to Pepperdine, the second to the Hotel where you are staying. Hope you got them both. You know your Aunt Beulah is living in El Cerrito. Is this any where near you? Gee, but I wish I could see you. Seems like such a long time since you left home. We are thinking about putting our property up for sale soon as we can clear it up a bit. Dad is working good now during this real cold spell. Well, Son, please try to make it on your very own. All things will work out for good because I know you love the Lord.

Bye, write us soon.

Lots of love,
Mom and Dad

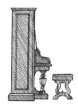

I'm Empty and Aching

It's a good song. And like most Simon and Garfunkel, you have to be in the right mood, and you have to *listen to the words*. I hadn't heard it in a long time – years and years. I was traveling – alone. An old ache had made me go back to Michigan – to my birthplace – to my old houses and neighborhoods – to my old schools and church buildings. I walked the hallways, sat in my old desks, stood in the pulpits, went to the locker rooms, walked across the fields. I was home again. All of the old names and faces slowly returned. Joe Vestrand, Bill Owen, Mary Jo Kirkwood, Romelda Waldron, Janet Ammerman, Barbara Bidwell, Ed Bartz, Susy Teller, Judy Ratner, Fred Nahabedian, John Hall, Clayton Middleton, and Roger Mumbrue. The giddy, exhilarating, unreasonable happiness – the sheer joy, the power and strength of youth – falling in love and being invincible – I tingled with it. And the pain, the rejection, the losses – the loneliness and bewilderment –

that came back too.

I went back on purpose. I wanted to find something that I had lost along the way – something I remembered – something I knew I once had – but I couldn't quite place it or give a name to it. It came to me at Wing Lake School on Fifteen Mile Road. Why there? – I don't know. I was only there part of one school year – my sixth-grade year.

But it came to me there.

The old section of the school – the section I attended – with the stone walls and the huge windows and the bell tower – is no longer used. But some thoughtful folks had preserved it. They gave me a key to my old classroom, and I went in – reverently. I found my old desk, and I sat down. I remembered my teacher, my good friend Floyd Eslinger, and I remembered the athletic contests. It's funny, Wing Lake School was the only place I ever played soccer – how weird.

As I sat there, alone, in the dead silence, I remembered Kitty Proctor – my first love. Sitting there thinking about that time and remembering blond-haired, blue-eyed Kitty Proctor – *it came to me*. You see, Kitty Proctor was not only my *first* serious and romantic love – she was the last. I mean she was the last girl I loved purely – *innocently* – before eros distorted my relationship with girls – and almost everything else as well. It was before I became selfish and manipulative in my girl relationships.

I went to the blackboard, and I wrote my name and the date, and I left this message.

> "I loved Kitty Proctor here.
> I loved her without her ever knowing it.
> I loved her purely – nobly –
> *innocently.*
> What I would give
> to have that feeling
> again."

Later, as I was driving between Royal Oak and Rochester, I listened to a tape, and it was Simon and Garfunkel and *America* – a song about two graduated high schoolers who go to look for America. They hitchhike and take buses. I remembered doing that too – I hitchhiked from Royal Oak, Michigan, to Los Angeles, California. But it wasn't America that I was looking for, and it's really not America that those two were after. The most poignant words are,

> " 'Kathy, I'm lost,' I said,
> though I knew she was sleeping.
> I'm empty and aching
> and I don't know why."

I remembered being empty and aching and not knowing why – and now, I'm very much older, and I still ache. In fact, it's sometimes worse – *but now I know why.*

> I want to be *innocent* again.
> I want to be free
> From my knowledge of evil,
> From the experience of sin.
> I want not to want to do bad things.
> I want to be *innocent* again.

Thoreau was right – most men do lead lives of quiet desperation, swimming upstream against a relentless current, seeking an harbor of safety from the evil that seeks to overwhelm us. It is *innocence* that motivates – impels us – driving us constantly on. We want to have the peace that is only found in purity.

That is why David cries,

> "Create in me a clean heart, oh God."
> —Psalm 51:10 ASV

And that is why Jesus says,

> "Blessed are the pure in heart:
> for they shall see God."
> —Matthew 5:8 ASV

And that is why the apostle Paul says,

> "To the pure,
> all things are pure,
> but to those who are corrupted . . .
> nothing is pure."
> —Titus 1:15 NIV

Coming
of Age

♦

122

FIVE

Home

Home – don't wait
too long to go back,
and don't get too far
away.

Home

Much has been written and said about home, and while most of it is true, it is also somehow inadequate. What I write here will also be inadequate. My memories of home are varied and complex because things changed so much.

I know you're in a hurry to get through this introduction and get to the stories — and really, you'd like to just skip this part. But I honestly think it would be worth your while to read it all the way through. I'd like you to pay special attention to the following questions. As you read them, put the book down and think about them — try hard to answer them honestly.

1. What memories of your home left lasting impressions? List five.
2. Did you like being there? Always? Almost always? Sometimes? Seldom?
3. Do you remember your parents as — Happy? Discontent? Worried? Ambitious? Religious?
4. What types of concerns dominated the conversation in your home? Finances? Spiritual matters? Politics? Jobs? Recreation? Community?
5. Would you say that the atmosphere of your home was — Relaxed? Tense? Boring? Eventful? Fun? Strict?
6. Do you want your home to be essentially similar to or substantially different from your parents' home?

Some of these questions you may be able to answer pretty quickly and easily. Some will take much longer, and the answers will be much less definitive. You will find yourself saying, "Well, it depends on when you mean," or "Well, sometimes it was — and sometimes. . . ." It's that way for me. I have memories of happy, carefree, contented times, and memories of troubled, confused, and frightening times. And sometimes, it all seems to blend together — which leaves me with an

appropriately obscure feeling.

We all have some ideas about what home should be. We put neat little plaques on our kitchen walls with nice little poems or sayings about home — and much of what they say is true. But there are those nagging discrepancies — between what home *should be* and what it *is* — that trouble us. *Real* homes are like *real* lives – all mixed up with goods and bads. It's just that in some homes, the good things outweigh the *bad* things. And when that happens, we say, "I had a great home" – but we quickly add – "Of course, there were a lot of bad times, too." When folks say that they had bad homes, most often they mean that their outstanding memories are bad – the good times and happy days have been overshadowed by negatives.

Most parents little realize the impact of memories on a child's mind. Lasting impressions are created by the most seemingly trivial occasions. I pray that as you read the stories in this book, that you will be impressed with how my whole notion about home was the result of situations that my parents had no idea would stay with me.

Although you cannot generate the specific situations that create lasting memories – you can control how you react to them. You also control *how much* time you spend together as family and *how* you spend it.

Home

♦

128

> You will not make lasting impressions
> and create sustaining memories
> watching television.

Parents are always telling me that they wish they had more family time. *What keeps them from it?* Is it jobs, social obligations, school activities, schedules, TV? Are those things out of your control? Of course not. They can be changed any time

> you have the courage and determination to do so.

Unfortunately, the time we do spend together as families is sometimes of such poor quality or so uneventful that *family time* is a negative thing. Parents are so physically and emotionally drained by their work and social obligations that they are irritable, detached, and unenthusiastic when family time comes. The result is that the kids might actually prefer less of it.

I do not mean that family time is supposed to be a thrill-a-minute ride through an amusement part – in fact, I mean the opposite. Trips to Disneyland, Sea World, or even the county fair can be cop-outs for parents who try to *create* good times by spending lots of money, *artificially* entertaining their children at no personal expense. I do mean that parents must *invest themselves* in their families – that family time can and must include quiet, thoughtful, meaningful moments – and that there must be a *drawing together.* You cannot artificially create that, but you can create an atmosphere – of caring and sharing –

> that allows it to happen.

Saying Grace

It was Kristen who really got me to thinking about it. We were eating lunch: Kristen, who was seventeen at the time; Lincoln, who was twenty-three; and I — older than both of them put together. You know, one of the really great things about getting older is that you reach a point where you will never again be twice as old as your kids — it's almost as good as getting younger — *almost*. Judi was at school (she's old, too, but we don't talk about it); Brendan, he was twenty, had gone to wheat harvest; Debbie, same age as Lincoln, was at work. We were sitting at the kitchen table and Lincoln said, "Well, I got to go," and he got up, stacked his dishes, and went to the sink.

"When did we stop saying, 'May I be excused?' " Kristen asked. At first, I thought she was just needling her brother — but it was a half-serious question — and although much time has passed —

it nags at me still.

You see, when the children were small, they had to be *excused* before they could leave the table. They were not allowed to sing, to interrupt, to talk excessively, or to leave the table — except in emergencies. If you left the table without permission, you didn't come back. Virtually every meal was a family experience that began with a prayer and ended with a "May I be excused?" There was a set time for dinner, and my wife planned and executed each meal. What was prepared was eaten by all –

even the peas.

Recently, I dropped by unexpectedly at the home of a couple I had been counseling. I was traveling through their neighborhood and remembered that I needed to mention something to them and thought I'd just drop by. They have serious family-marital problems. The husband answered the door and invited me in. It was mealtime – except there was no meal. I mean, there was no plan – no coming together. The mother flew between the can opener, the refrigerator, the cupboard, and the microwave. The oldest boy took what he wanted to the living room to watch the TV, which was blaring away. The youngest boy roamed aimlessly around the table, stuffing his mouth full of whatever he could reach. The girl sort of came and went like a squirrel, who takes a nut and disappears, then returns for another. The mother never sat down, and the father – oblivious to the turmoil – visited with me over the noise of the TV.

Nobody passed anything.
They did not talk to each other.
They did not say grace.

It is not for nothing that the apostle Paul tells us that God is not the author of confusion – not in the church, not in society, and not in the home. Rather, he is the source of order, and he expects his people to lead orderly lives. When we refuse to live according to his nature, confusion and loss of identity result.

How is it possible for us to have meaningful family relationships in the midst of chaos? I submit that under the conditions I have described, there is no "family," because the sense of order that is necessary to define the relationships is missing.

Saying grace was more important than I ever knew as a child. It was an open, practical, personal, and group acknowledgment of our need and his presence. It provided an atmosphere of order and set the tone for our time together. It was a moment of quiet and of peace. As we joined hands around the table, we were reminded that we were one – a family – and that God was integral to our family. As we passed the potatoes and the peas, we listened to each other and learned unconsciously about what a family is. If Dad talked about his job or the men he worked with, he became more real to us. If he and Mom talked about the church or politics or the neighbors, our eyes were opened to a larger world, and our family took its place in that world. Each of us commented on his or her day – specific questions were asked, information was given – but more than that, ties were formed, and we had family consciousness.

We came to know that we were Smiths – Fred Smiths to be exact. And we learned that there were things that Fred Smiths did and did not do. Being a Fred Smith meant that we did not take what was not ours or what we had not earned. We obeyed authority. We told the truth. The teacher was right. Everything comes from God. You stick up for your family. You help your neighbors when they need it. You mind your own business. You never eat without washing your hands, face, and behind your ears – I never did understand why I had to wash behind my ears –

I still don't.

We learned that Fred Smiths don't buy Ford automobiles or vote for Democrats. We learned that "life is not fair," "there is no such thing as luck," and "we should never miss a chance to keep our mouths shut."

As Smiths we believed in certain things and not in others, and we took satisfaction in our identity. One thing I always knew – Fred Smiths always say grace before they eat, and before they leave the table they say, "May I be excused?"

My notions of home were deeply founded and well defined. When I was grown and married, I knew what my job was and what a home was supposed to be.

What has sustained my family is the fact that during my children's formative years, I adhered to my own raising. I copied the format of my father's house. Kristen's question reminded me that at some point we began losing that. I don't know if we could have salvaged more of it or not, maybe the price seemed too high – or it was just easier to give in to social conventions. I do know it has cost us much in terms of what we cannot replace, and sometimes we are in such a hurry or so fragmented that we do not say grace or "May I be excused?" I wonder what pattern my children will adhere to as they raise their families.

Will they say grace?
Will they say, "May I be excused?"
Will they know what their job is and
what a home is supposed to be?

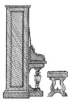

I Must Get Home

"Home is the place where,
when you have to go there,
They have to take you in."

"I should have called it
Something you somehow haven't to deserve."
—Robert Frost, *Death of the Hired Man*

Home

♦

132

I have killed many rabbits. I suspect ten thousand or more. That seems an incredible number, but I have hunted them for forty years, and on many occasions have killed in excess of twenty-five in a single day. It is worth noting that out of all those rabbits, I remember only two as single incidents. This story is about one of them. I shot this particular rabbit near Evansville, Indiana, on a farm that belonged to the family of Mary Lois Branstedder (now Mary Lois Moore). I was hunting with my good friend and brother, Al Strykowski, and it was a cold, overcast day with much fresh snow on the ground.

We were hunting along a brushy creek bank. The rabbit, I suppose, had been searching for food, and when I came too close, it darted from its cover. It was just a shadow – seen – not seen – flitting through small trees and brush. I fired – missed – fired again and scored. I saw it tumble, head over heels.

I found the place where the shotgun pellets had made long, linear tracings through the snow; found the spot where the stricken rabbit had rolled headlong; found the tiny, perfectly round, red spots of blood soaking and spreading in the snow; found where the rabbit had righted itself and begun its floundering attempt to escape. It was obvious that its powerful rear legs were broken, and the rabbit was dragging itself by its front legs – tunneling through the snow. I tracked it as best I could in the dense cover, even glimpsing it now and then –

but I could not catch it.

I ultimately tracked it to a hole in the creek bank, obviously its home. It was lying, completely exhausted – dying, within my reach. As I pulled it out, it made a single last attempt to resist by pawing with its front legs. And then it uttered what I have only heard on two subsequent occasions – a high-pitched wail – a sound so shrill, so filled with despair and hopelessness – so like the forlorn cry of a mother for a lost child – so eerie and haunting that I dropped the rabbit as if I had gripped a red-hot coal. It made no further move or sound, and when I picked it up again, it was dead. I was so moved by the event – it made such a profound impression on me –

that I shot no more rabbits that day.

I wonder, yet, at the powerful, instinctive drive of the dying rabbit to get home. I thought at first that the rabbit was just trying to get away from me, but that wasn't it at all. It had no thoughts for me – it had only one thought,

"I must get home."

It had just enough strength to get home – and no more. And when it got there, it made no attempt to go farther – *home* was the only balm it knew, and if home could not heal, healing was not to be found. Death alone could erase its pain. And that last despairing cry – how I shudder at the hopelessness – the horror of the warning it sounded to all other rabbits.

Home

"Don't wait too long," it said,
"and don't get too far away."

I couldn't help thinking about those times when I was stricken, bleeding, exhausted, and bewildered. At those times, I had only one thought –

"I must get home."

♦

133

And home was always there. What if I had arrived and found it gone – the family scattered, no warmth, no welcome, no forwarding address.

Home – what a holy, sacred word that is. Praise God for those who stay by the firesides – keep a light in the window, a bed with clean sheets, a good smell coming from the kitchen, and a "We've been waiting for you." What a noble task, what a high calling of God – surely, there is some place of special recognition before the throne of the Most High for those who build and sustain homes – and just as surely and sadly – a special place, away from his presence, for those who defile and destroy them.

Home.
Don't wait too long to go back,
and don't get too far away.

Don't forget, parents and grandparents, when *you* have lost all hope, there may be a lost, hurting, despairing child out there who is saying,

"I must get home."

Today Is My Birthday

When I was small, birthdays were much anticipated events – especially *my* birthday. Somehow or other, after I turned fifty, I began to wish that folks would forget my birthday. At this stage of aging, I simply cannot – for the life of me – understand why anyone would want to celebrate getting older.

My mother always tried to make my birthdays special by having a party. She allowed me to invite all my friends. She would make my favorite cake and fix my favorite foods – and of course there were presents. We might even have ice cream. And naturally, they sang "Happy Birthday," and I made a wish and blew out the candles – with one breath, of course – and then they clapped. I felt very special on my birthday, and the fact that my family celebrated it made me know that they were glad I was born and that they wanted me. Of course, I didn't think about that at the time, and nobody told me that that was what it meant –

but somehow I knew.

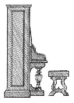

Back in 1989 I was flying from somewhere to somewhere, and as you know, you can't fly from somewhere to anywhere without going through Dallas or Atlanta. I had a three-hour layover between flights in Dallas – now, if you did that to a dog they would arrest you for cruel and unusual punishment. I was desperate for entertainment. I had read on the plane until my eyes were watering, so I called home to talk to my wife. She said, "Hi honey, I'm sure glad you called. Sue is in the driveway waiting on me. I hope you have a good trip – bye." It may not have been quite that brutal, but you get the idea. The call lasted about three minutes – I had two hours and fifty-seven minutes to go.

I started walking – not to anywhere, just ambling along. As I ambled, I began to read all the overhead signs: Baggage Claim, Gates 3–11, Ground Transportation, Restaurants, Emergency Exit, Restrooms, Barber Shop, Phones – all with the appropriate directional arrows. Then I saw one that I hadn't seen before – it said Chapel. What sort of chapel do you find in an airport? I wondered. I didn't have anything else to do, so I allowed my intrigue to lead me to follow the arrows, and about a mile-and-a-half later, I found myself in a very small, plain room about fifteen feet square. There were straight-backed chairs against three of the walls and a library table in the middle with about fourteen Bibles of various sorts on top. With the exception of the back wall, which was stained glass, the room was indecorous to the point of monastic austerity.

I sat down. It was so quiet after the chaotic confusion of the terminal that the silence was unnerving. I prayed for a while, then picked up several of the Bibles and read short passages from each. I noticed a plaque on the wall that said the chapel was the result of a grant from the Meadows Foundation. I don't know who they are, but I'm indebted to the Meadows for

that quiet place of prayer.

Under the plaque was a guest register – like you see at a wedding or funeral – and I thought that was nice, so I signed my name. They had provided a space in the register for people to write down their thoughts, and I wrote down that I appreciated the thoughtfulness of the folks who provided the room. You know, when I finished writing I thought, "Boy, writing in this book is dumb. Nobody will ever go through this book and read what people wrote." It made me feel kind of sad, because some people had written quite a bit. So I thought I would read it, and then it wouldn't have been a waste of time.

It was fascinating – the things people had shared on those pages. They were really honest because they believed no one would ever see it – and if they did, it wouldn't matter because they wouldn't know who they were. Most of what was written showed the unmistakable signs of loneliness, grief, lostness, and frustration with life. One was particularly sad. It said,

> "Today is my birthday.
> I am stranded here alone.
> God help me to get home –
> and help them to want me."

I wonder if he got home? I wonder if they wanted him when he got there? Isn't that what we all want – to get home? And isn't that what you want – to be wanted?

Home is where you're wanted – it's where they celebrate your birthday to tell you that you're special. Home is supposed to be the kind of place that a child wants to come back to. It's the kind of place that's supposed to give us all a preview of the home God has prepared for us.

What a "Welcome Home" celebration God has planned. We will see our "birthday cake" – with just one giant candle. The angelic host will join with the redeemed in a celestial rendition of "Happy Birthday," and then we get to blow out the candle – with one breath, of course – and the clapping will be deafening. And then we will realize that all the things we ever wished have come true – that we are finally and forever home – and that we are wanted. There will be a great voice – like the sound of many waters – and it will say:

> "Welcome home.
> Today is your birthday."

♦

Going to Heaven

It was Christmas, 1987. We lived at 5420 28th Street in Lubbock, Texas. It's funny how thoughts – ideas – come to your mind – often totally unbidden and under the most ordinary circumstances.

I had been hunting with Lincoln and Brendan – out near Bovina – and with Scott and Charles Johnson. It had been a cold – very windy – whatelse-would-it-be-in-West-Texas – day, and we had had a successful hunting trip. We got home after dark, and I was in the utility room cleaning pheasants. Like the wind in West Texas, some things never change. It's true that I had killed *nearly* all the birds, but I was cleaning *every one*. Where were my boys? Their enthusiasm for hunting never did extend to cleaning the game, and so as soon as we hit the driveway, they had very important plans – in this case, showers, phone calls, and wrapping presents.

I was alone in the utility room, but sounds of activities in other parts of the house drifted in. I don't know how long it was before I became conscious of the symphonic blending. In the living room Kristen was playing "Moonlight Sonata," and in the family room Judi was putting ornaments on the tree – the boys were giving her advice while they wrapped presents. They were laughing and talking.

There were good smells coming from the kitchen, and I was overwhelmed by an unparalleled feeling of wholeness – completeness – and I didn't mind cleaning the pheasants.

"This is home," I thought.
"God, how I love this feeling."

And I felt just a tinge of sadness, because I knew it was passing away –

I could not hold it.

Going to heaven – being at home with God – became so important to me at that moment. I thought, "Dear God, please don't let me lose this." I don't think I'll clean pheasants there – somehow the idea of killing anything doesn't click with my concept of a home with God – but I don't have any problems imagining that Kris will play "Moonlight Sonata," and I'm sure we'll continue to wrap presents and sing "Silent Night" and celebrate the birth of our Lord.

Heaven is being able to hold those precious moments of wholeness forever; it is our

eternal *home*.

Home

♦

SIX

Humor

May God help us
to laugh – and to
enjoy the instant
release that
laughter brings.

Humor

There are few parenting tools that equal the value of a sense of humor. Few things in life can take the tension from the atmosphere – change disaster into victory – restore wounded pride – relieve the burden of guilt – and bring people into closer union – than genuine, good-natured laughter.

The ability to see what is humorous is a gift of God. Human beings are ridiculous, and if we could only let our pride down for a moment and have a good laugh at ourselves, we could heal more woes with humor than with a thousand psychoanalysts.

These next stories are simply indicative of the types of situations – most of them very serious at the time – which, viewed from a more distant perspective, are truly funny and deserve laughter much more than chagrin. May God help us, even at the moment, to laugh – and to teach our children the value of laughter, how to laugh at themselves, and how to enjoy the instant release that laughter brings.

Jary and the Belt

My sister, Jary, is the best person I ever knew, and she has had a remarkable effect on my life for good. I never knew her to do anything wrong – or even to think a wrong thought – which put considerable pressure on me, because

I did much of both.

Anyway, she is a remarkable person. I don't mean that I thought this when I was a kid – or that it was always sweetness and light between us – or even that I loved her for her gracious attempts to help me with my manners, my dress, my speech, my homework, my friends, my conduct – in church, at school, and everywhere else – brushing my teeth, taking more baths, combing my hair, cleaning my room – and every other area of my personal conduct.

Now, there you go – I know what you're thinking. You're thinking I was a slob, a recalcitrant deadbeat. Well, you're dead wrong, I wasn't nearly that bad – I may have been a slob, but I wasn't a deadbeat – it's just that some folks have more refined notions of propriety than others.

Take my belt, for instance.

♦

If you'll be patient, I'll try to make this worth your while. You see, I had this great belt – I got it from my Uncle Art, who was an alcoholic. When I got it, it was about twenty-two and one-half inches too long for my girth (that's the distance around your waist, in case you don't read much), but it never bothered me in the least. I was proud of that belt. It was handier than a whistle on a plow. When I was bored or trying to impress the girls, I would just unlimber that extra *twenty-one inches,* and I would twirl it while I whistled "Yankee Doodle." (I know you're wondering what happened to the other inch and a half of my belt. Of course you're supposed to be wondering about that; that's the reason I wrote "twenty-one inches" in italics – italics means that the print looks like this – *italics* – instead of like this – italics. Isn't it amazing what you can learn in books like this? Anyway, in order to find out what happened to the other inch and a half of my belt, you'll have to wait till the next story.)

I thought that twirling that belt was just about the neatest thing ever imagined, and many of the girls my age thought so too. Why, Becky Swarthout told me one time that it made her stomach turn over when she watched me – which I took as a high compliment. But my sister didn't see it that way – no, her jealousy caused her to have a coronary every time. She was mortified, embarrassed, and humiliated. "Look, Mom, he's doing it again." And, of course,

my mother always saw her side of it.

To shorten this story, let me tell you that they plotted against me, and played the dirtiest trick you can imagine. One day I was standing as nonchalantly as possible, leaning against the doorjamb in the kitchen, twirling my belt and whistling "Yankee Doodle" for all I was worth. I wasn't trying to impress anybody – there was nobody to impress. I was doing it for the absolute joy I got out of aggravating people. You wouldn't believe it possible, but my very own mother sort of sidled up beside me, grabbed me suddenly, and pinned my arms to my sides. My sister, then, came up behind me, tripped me, and wrestled me to the floor. And as I lay screaming bloody murder, they cut off that extra twenty-one inches of my belt –

with a butcher knife.

Any psychologist worth half his salt could have a picnic with this tale and could explain much of my unusual behavior in later life – based on that emotional trauma inflicted upon me in my formative years. It was like a death. I mourned the loss of my belt for at least thirty-two years. I kept the piece they cut off – for nearly a week – and then discovered that it made an excellent pocket for a slingshot I was making.

Trimming Spot's Tail

I'm sure you've been waiting with breathless anticipation to find out what happened to the other inch and a half of my belt. Well, I lost that inch and a half in an accident. You see, we had this dog named Spot – he was solid black. Why did we call him Spot? Because he looked like one – that's why. Spot had an unusually long, heavy, shaggy, black tail, that didn't seem to go with his body. I think that is because Spot's ancestry was a little doubtful. His parents were undoubtedly fine, upstanding dogs in their own right, but I don't think they were registered with the American Kennel Society – but Spot didn't care and neither did I. Spot's tail was troublesome. He wagged it constantly, and it knocked stuff off of tables, and it got long black hair on your trousers and the furniture –

and it looked weird.

I mean, anybody who saw Spot for the first time would make some comment about his tail. It was a little embarrassing. My dad finally decided that Spot was developing a persecution complex because of his tail and that he would be much better off – and so would we – if about half of his tail was cut off. He decided to wrap my belt around Spot's tail, to keep it from bleeding too much, and to sort of serve as a marker for where he wanted to make his cut.

I thought we might ought to sort of consult Spot on this matter, because it worried me that a tail amputation might be a little traumatic, sort of unsettling – painful even. But my father assured me that dogs don't have much feeling in their tails – I wished I had thought to ask him how he came by that knowledge before we had the operation – because afterward it wasn't important. Anyway –

I felt a lot better.

It was quite an event; all my friends came over – it isn't every day that you have a tail amputation, you know. I could have sold tickets if I'd been thinking. Everybody was making over Spot, petting him and playing with him, and Spot was so excited by all the attention that he was running and jumping, nearly turning himself inside out making friends with the whole gang and getting long, black hair on everybody. He didn't know that his tail sacrifice was the main event of the day.

We stood around in a circle, and we laid old Spot down and stretched out his tail on a two-by-four – it looked like a big, black sausage – with hair. I was holding Spot's head, and I told him what my dad had told me about dogs not having any feeling in their tails, but it didn't seem to help Spot feel better – like it had me. Spot just lay there, sort of quivering –

he knew something was up.

My father was determined to do his work with one whack, so he raised the ax high above his head and took careful aim. I think that right at that moment, he might have wavered a little in his resolution, because he paused when the ax reached its highest point – but with all of us standing there watching him, he sort of had to see it through. I was stroking Spot's head and talking to him – reassuring him that this would only take a minute, it wouldn't hurt at all – and even if it did, it would be worth it because we'd all be happier afterward.

I don't think Spot was listening to me. I think that out of the corner of his eye, he saw my dad – standing over him with that ax raised in a threatening position. From Spot's vantage point, it may not have been exactly clear what my father was aiming at. As the ax descended, old Spot yelped like he'd been stung by the Great White Hornet – and he jumped. My dad almost missed – but not quite. He cut off seven inches of Spot's tail –

and an inch and a half of my belt.

In spite of my father's assurance that dogs have no feelings in their tails, Spot sure did take on. It may have just been an act – to gain sympathy – but he shot around the yard, yelping and howling like all the demons in hell were after him. I never saw a dog take on so. He even tried to bite where his tail used to be – which was hilarious to us –

but Spot didn't seem to think so.

Now you would think that he would have been grateful for all the attention that we showered upon him, plus the fact that he had been made more agreeable to us at very little expense to himself – he wasn't. That fool dog became very suspicious of us. I never did understand it. He never allowed my father to come within ten feet of him again as long as he lived, and every time anybody picked up the ax – old Spot left the yard so fast that he didn't get traction for three hundred yards, and he didn't come back for three days. I think he even resented me for laughing at his antics –

which was totally unreasonable.

You know, we're always willing to make changes in other folks so as to make them more agreeable to us. We are quite willing to amputate anything in them which we find offensive. We nearly always assume that it won't bother them, because they don't have any feelings in that area, anyway. We say,

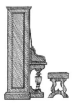

"I'll love you if . . ."
"I'll accept you when . . ."
"You can be a part of our group if . . ."

and always what's implied is that something about you must be amputated, because *we* don't like it. And then we wonder why folks are suspicious of us or give us the cold shoulder. Maybe they see that ax raised high in the air, and they're not too sure of just what we're aiming at. "This won't hurt a bit" and "We'll all be happier after"

somehow doesn't seem to help,
either.

Don't Worry, Be Happy

I was working in the yard when I remembered that I had promised a friend of mine that I would call him. Because I was dirty and sweaty, I went to the kitchen phone. When I picked it up, the line was dead. This was not an unusual happening in a house that has at least twelve phones and three kids, so I began searching for a phone with the receiver off the hook.

In the family room, the TV was on — but no one was in the room. As I approached the kids' bedrooms, I felt the floors vibrating and observed that the wall hangings were swaying precariously. My daughter's stereo was blasting away, and on her bed, right in front of the stereo, was a phone with the receiver off. All the lights were on in her room, but there was no one there.

She was in the shower.
I was ticked.

"Your stereo is on!" I screamed at the bathroom door. There was no response. I opened the door so I could be heard and was almost suffocated by the steam. Through the fog, I saw a red light glowing dimly on the sink, and I heard a familiar, high-pitched humming. Her curling iron was on, and her hair dryer was running. From behind the shower door, I heard her singing the words to some song I didn't know had words, but the refrain is,

"Don't worry, be happy."

"Your stereo is on," my voice was like a trumpet in the confined quarters.

"What?" she said. "I can't hear you, Dad – turn my stereo down" – and she sang – "Don't worry, be happy."

I went to her room and turned the stereo off, put the receiver back on the phone, and returned – but I was not happy.

"Kristen!" I said in a mild shout.

"You don't have to yell, Dad; I can hear you. What do you want?"

"Why is your stereo on?" I said with great intensity – less volume.

"I wanted to listen to it while I was in the shower; you can turn it off if you want to. And Dad, while you're in the bedroom, would you see if Wendi is still on the phone. She wanted to listen to a tape of mine, so I left the receiver off for her," and then she resumed her singing. "Don't worry, be happy."

There was tension, frustration, and a measure of unbelief in my voice.

"Will – you – stop – singing – that – stupid – song? Let me see if I have this right? The reason the phone in the kitchen is dead is because Wendi has been listening to a tape of yours over the phone, while you are in the shower? Good grief! Do you have any idea how ridiculous that is?"

"It's not ridiculous, Dad; it's a generation-gap thing. She's probably hung up by now, anyway, so you can use it if you like. Oh, hey, Dad, have you seen my shoes?"

"Oh, hey, yourself," I said. "Don't change the subject. I'm still on the phone thing."

"Why do you have to make a federal case out of everything. I told you; it's just a simple case of generation gap."

"It's more a case of the *gap* between your ears, which leads me to the question about your shoes. Which pair are you looking for? There's one in every room. By the way, I suppose there's a generation-gap answer as to why the TV is on?"

"Yeah," she said, "I'm watching a neat program on the Discovery Channel."

"Do you think I'm an idiot? You're in the shower – you're not watching anything but steam! Do you know how long you've been in there?"

"No, but I'm sure you do."

"Do you know what the purpose of a shower is? It is not to provide the atmosphere for "light entertainment." The purpose of a shower is to remove dirt from the body, and once that is accomplished – which I figure should never take more than three minutes because you take one three times a day – in spite of the fact that I have never witnessed you doing one, single thing to get dirty – which is another generation-gap thing, I'm sure. Hey, maybe I just figured out why you take so long – you're looking for something to wash off. Anyway – once you have done that, you're supposed to get out. Do you know how much it costs to heat water?"

"You mean that hot water costs more than cold water? – Go figure that! I mean, it all comes out of the same faucet. How does the water company know if you're using hot or cold water? Does it cost less if you mix it up? Please don't explain it – it's another generation-gap thing, I'm sure. Besides, you've made your point. I'll be right out – and the TV is on because I didn't want to have to wait for the picture tube to warm up. Does it cost more to warm it up than to leave it on? Just kidding – don't worry, be happy."

"While we're on this topic, did you know that your curling iron is on and your hair dryer is running?"

"Could we get off this topic? It doesn't promote positive parent-child relationships *or* bridge the generation gap."

"Don't give me that junk about positive parent-child relationships – if you want some of that, try demonstrating some re–spon–si–bil–i–ty – I repeat, why is your hair dryer running and your curling iron on?"

"You see, here is a perfectly good example of the generation gap – when you were my age, they hadn't been invented yet, so you don't understand. How much over a hundred are you? Just kidding. Actually, there's a perfectly understandable reason for that. I'm in a hurry, and I don't want to wait for them to heat up when I get out of the shower. And hey, Dad, could you leave me ten bucks? I'm going out for pizza with my friends tonight.

Don't worry, be happy."

"You're in a *hurry?* When did you start being in a hurry? Your curling iron and hair dryer are hot *now!* – and so am I! I have the distinct feeling that everything I have said has gone up the vent with the steam from the hot water."

"Oh, Dad, you're just jealous because you don't need a hair dryer or curling iron – you got nothing to dry or curl! Take it easy – just a little levity to take the tension out of this conversation. I heard every word you said – it made a lasting impression. You need to relax, Dad; you're all tight – you know – like *tight* – you need to remember – don't worry, be happy."

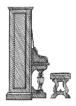

"Tight! – you think I'm tight! You haven't seen me tight – my precious – but you are *going* to see me tight! Let me tell *you* something about the generation gap – *tight* – in my somewhat outdated, generation-gap vocabulary means –

not free with money.

You *do* understand money – right? Your pizza money just went to pay the hot water and electric bill. How's that for bridging

the generation gap?"

There was a very pronounced silence behind the shower curtain. For the first time since this conversation began, I had the feeling that I had her undivided attention – that something I said finally registered. There is still one thing that brings the generations together –

money!

I felt so much better as I turned to walk out that I couldn't refrain from singing – just loud enough to be heard –

"Don't worry, be happy."

A Continual Dripping

"A quarrelsome wife is like
a constant dripping on a rainy day;
restraining her is like restraining the wind
or grasping oil with the hand."
—Proverbs 27:15–16 NIV

In 1951 or '52 my father bought a 1950 Buick. I remember it well because it was the car that I eventually learned to drive in. The engine was a straight eight, and the body was green. It was also huge. There was enough

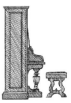

*H*umor

♦

153

room in the backseat to put a kitchen table and chairs for people to sit in and play cards. It must have weighed more than an elephant.

My mother was an excellent driver, but whenever my dad was in the car – he drove. When Mom drove, she was very calm and confident – when Dad drove, she was a "nervous wreck" (pun intended). She made little hissing noises when he turned corners, and she wore the carpet out and made indentations in the steel under her feet, pushing on the floorboard when Dad didn't apply the brakes fast enough to suit her. When he passed a car, she sort of moaned and writhed in her seat. She also gave him a steady stream of "sound advice and helpful hints" to keep him alert.

It never affected him much.

I guess that over the years he just tuned her out and drove pretty much like he wanted to. Occasionally – when she began to get on his nerves – he'd switch on the radio and raise the volume to a level appropriate to the decibels she was putting out. Mom was relentless, but my dad would keep his fingers on the volume control until she would have to give it up.

It sure brought the color to the back of her neck.

♦

Much of the weather in Michigan is not conducive to safe driving. There is much fog, rain, snow, ice, and slush. We drove several miles to church, and since the weather never interfered with our going – my dad drove in the worst of conditions.

From my backseat observation post, I witnessed much hissing, writhing, moaning, foot stomping and heard much conflicting advice:

"Slow down, Fred!"

"Go faster, or we'll be late!"

"You're too close to the middle, Fred!"

"Don't run off the edge!"

"Watch that car!"

"Keep your eyes on the road, Fred."

And my dad drove on – completely impervious to her instructions and occasionally reaching for the radio knob. It was the best entertainment of every week, and I always hoped the weather would be bad because good driving conditions sure took the fun out of going to church.

Although he never stopped her advice giving completely, he sure slowed her down some because of the following incident.

Driving under the type of weather conditions I mentioned earlier inevitably leads to much slipping and sliding, especially with the road conditions of the fifties. Most of that slipping is completely harmless, and people who drive in those conditions regularly accept it and accommodate themselves to it quite naturally.

My mother had read somewhere about a family that had lost control of their car and in the subsequent crash had been trapped inside. When the car caught fire – they all burned to death. She developed a terrible, psychotic paranoia about being trapped in a car. Every time our car slipped – even slightly – she would gasp, grab the door handle, open it, and get ready to bail out if the car continued to slide.

No amount of reasoning could stop her.

One night in early spring, we were returning home from church in Rochester in a wet, blinding snowstorm. My mother had stepped up both the quantity, quality, and volume of her advice, and she was very tense. Somewhere between Square Lake Road and Sylvan Glen Golf Course, my dad lost control of the car. He wasn't going fast – there was no other traffic – and we were in absolutely no danger at all. The big Buick began to spin slowly around and around in the road. It finally headed backwards and sideways toward the shallow ditch on the opposite side of the road. Before we could stop her, my mother opened the door and bailed out. She slid ahead of the car, into the ditch –

and the Buick slid right over her.

My dad and I were sure she was dead, and we jumped out and ran to her. Much to our relief, she was completely unhurt, but quite uncomfortable, laying in the freezing water and wet snow. The Buick was right on top of her, and we could not get her out. There simply was not room. We knew she was all right, because we could still hear her muffled voice continuing her tirade about my dad's driving and his failure to heed her good advice, which was why she was where she was.

While she fumed, my dad and I discussed how best to extricate her. I thought we might try driving the car forward and up the ditch bank, but my dad said that was no good because the bank might cave in. Then I suggested that we jack the car up high enough to make room to slide her out. My dad said that the jack would just sink in the mud. He said that he guessed we'd have to walk to town and get a wrecker that could lift the car.

It was a long way to town,

and I wondered how Mom was going to take the waiting, but I began to catch something in his voice, and when I looked at him, he winked at me. "We'll be back in no more than an hour, Florence," he said. "You just rest easy."

My mother had become extremely quiet during this last discussion, but now she spoke clearly. "Fred Smith, you get me out of here, and you get me out of here this minute," she said.

"Well, Florence," he said, "have you got any advice on how I might do that?"

The silence from under the car was broken only by the furious grinding of her mental wheels as they searched frantically for an answer. "No!" she finally snapped.

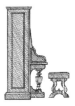

Humor

◆

155

"Well," my dad said, in a very satisfied tone, "imagine that. You know, I just remembered that shovel I keep in the trunk to shovel snow at the church."

He opened the trunk, got the shovel, and in ten minutes had made a hole big enough for her to crawl out. She was a mess – soaking wet, freezing cold, covered with mud, and quite miserable. My dad put his suit coat around her, and we got into the comfortable warmth of the big Buick and drove home.

You know, my mother never tried jumping out of the car again; rather, whenever the car slipped, she would move closer to my dad. She also gave no driving advice on the way home that night – in fact, she never recovered her old form.

It sure did take the fun out of going to church.

Humor

♦

SEVEN

Winning and Losing

When you're all alone and
you're getting scored on
and you can't stop them –
it means a lot to know
that it doesn't matter to
those who love you.

Winning and Losing

Sports are important. I could wish that they were not so important as they have become, but there is no doubt that they impact family life dramatically. Even fifty years ago, in my rural community of Troy, Michigan, sports were important. At every church picnic there was a hotly contested all-afternoon softball game. At my little three-room school, I played baseball and marbles. In the winters we had ice skating and sledding – both of which were highly competitive, especially ice skating. We played tag, red-rover red-rover, crack the whip, and ice hockey, which became my second athletic passion – baseball was my first. Later, when we moved to town, it was football, then basketball, golf, and tennis. I learned the exhilaration of competition all too soon, and my life was totally dominated for years with concepts of –

winning and losing.

There have been many positive experiences for me in sports, many memorable occasions, but I caution you that the overall impact has probably been negative. My life has been terribly unbalanced by athletics, and I have wandered farther from the Kingdom of God because of sports, than because of any other single facet of my life, save one.

As parents, you will make lasting impressions on your children in this area – as spectators, as supporters, and as participants. Athletic parents not only display their *true natures* when they play, but also when they watch and as they drive home. Lectures on sportsmanship, correct attitudes, being a good loser – and on maintaining balance relative to outcomes, the judges' decisions, and luck – aren't really worth much

if your *conduct* belies your words.

I freely confess to you that in no area have I failed my children and myself to a greater degree than in this one. I could write many stories about my actions as a spectator, player, and coach – when my children were in the audience or even participating with me – that have left a lasting impression on them. I am glad that those moments are not on video, because my *actions*

161

Winning and Losing

♦

162

were totally out of harmony with what they have heard me *teach* — all of their lives.

To our children, we are always parents — at home, at work, on the athletic field, at church, or driving down the highway. Again, I remind you that *consistency between behavior and teaching is what counts.* It's how you react under pressure that is important, and it's almost impossible to plan for those moments, because they come so unexpectedly. I think the most outstanding thing about my parents' attitude toward my athletic endeavors was their almost total neutrality. I do not remember my mother ever attending an athletic contest I was involved in, except one junior high baseball game. Sports, to my mother, was not something to waste a great deal of time on — time that could better be spent stocking the grocery shelves at the B & C Market or anyplace else I could find a job.

My father was not quite as negative, and he came to several of my games and sometimes even to practice — especially football. He never got involved, though — he wasn't a booster club member or anything. I honestly can't remember him saying anything, pro or con, except a very quiet, "That was a good game," or "I'm sorry you lost." The only exception to that was my involvement in ice hockey, which is a story of its own that I will write down one day.

Looking back, I think their attitude was a healthy one. If they had been rabid fans, real cheerleaders who allowed their lives and schedules to be dominated by physicals, uniform fittings, practice schedules, games, and booster club activities, I believe it would have made it even worse for me. As it was — the little balance I maintained was probably due to the very casual, offhanded attitude they took. If my games fit into their schedule, fine — if not, I was on my own.

I hope that these stories will give you a perspective on athletics that perhaps you haven't had before.

I hope you will laugh
and cry
and think —
and be better.

Cross-Country

My son Lincoln ran cross-country in high school. He wasn't a spectacular runner, although he was a determined one. I think he ran his best in
nearly every race. He only won one race that I remember, but I was pleased
with his dedication and his effort, and I felt that the rigorous training was
especially good for him. I attended every meet that I could.

There was another boy on the team, a close friend of Lincoln's, who was
a gifted runner. I will call him Tim. He had red hair and a great smile, and
I liked him. His father was a very successful businessman in town, who
dressed very stylishly and drove flashy cars. In a town as small as ours,

you couldn't help but notice things like that.

Most cross-country races involved more than two schools, and the one I
want to tell you about was no exception. I don't remember how many
schools were involved; I do remember that there was a much larger turnout
than normal, because everybody was interested in the matchup between
Tim and another state-class athlete – a Mexican-American boy from a
neighboring town.

I still remember the marked contrast between the two boys. Tim – very
tall and slender, very fair, red headed, with long, smooth, powerful strides,
and the Mexican-American boy – dark skinned, dark haired, short, stocky,
with quick, almost jerky strides.

Tim's dad was there. He had come early. He parked his expensive auto-mobile close to the start and finish lines, pulled off his suit coat, and stood visiting with other local dignitaries.

The course was a beautiful one. It began and ended on a hilltop, which overlooked a vast section of high desert. With binoculars you could see approximately three-fourths of the course. The race began with the runners charging down off of that hilltop — a very sharp descent — for at least two hundred yards — then breaking off into the plateau of rocks, cactus, and desert scrub.

It was easy to see Tim. Even when he was a long way off, you could see the sun on that red hair and white body. He was leading, but he had a dark shadow — never too far away. Every watcher forgot the other runners as they watched the magnificent dual between these opposites.

When they reached the bottom of the long, daunting incline, which led to the finish line, Tim was twenty or thirty feet ahead — a comfortable lead — but the Mexican-American boy had apparently planned his race that way. With a supreme effort, he made up over half the distance that separated them before Tim became aware that he was making a move. Both boys were nearing exhaustion, and Tim's attempt to increase his speed to hold off his challenger was feeble. Only five feet separated them as they came within thirty yards of the finish. Tim's father and the rest of the crowd had moved down the hill — everyone yelling encouragement to their champion.

The boys legs were heavy, they looked as if they were moving in slow motion. They felt, I'm sure, that they were going pretty fast, but I could have easily outrun either of them that last thirty yards. They had already given their best in outdistancing all other competitors.

It is a marvelous thing to be able to stand that close — to be within touch-ing distance, to actually *feel* the effort, the emotion, to be able to see every drop of sweat, every muscle movement, every line of the face, to *feel* the agony, the grim determination —

it was magnificent.

Tim was going to lose; I could sense it. The Mexican-American boy had more energy left, and his short, quick stride was more suited to the uphill grade than Tim's. I think Tim sensed it too, and the pain in his face was heartbreaking. He was doing his best —

but he had nothing left to give.

His dad was running beside him, red-faced with anger, heedless of the spectacle he made. He screamed, "Don't you let that boy beat you!" The last thirty yards seemed to last forever, but it ended. The Mexican-American boy passed Tim five yards from the finish line – less than two feet separated the winner and the loser.

They crossed the finish line, and both boys sagged in absolute exhaustion, surrounded by coaches, officials, family, and well wishers – with one exception. Tim's father had gone directly to his car and left in disgust. There was no smile, no embrace, no "I'm proud of you" or "What a great race! You'll get him next time." There was no encouragement, no laughter, no coming together. Tim's dad missed a great moment, a great opportunity –

one that is seldom repeated.

A few minutes later, Lincoln came in. I ran up the hill beside him. He was as exhausted as any of those ahead of him. He had given his best. Less than two minutes separated him from the winners – a very small space in the length of a lifetime.

Sports bring out the best and the worst in parents –
what do they bring out in you?

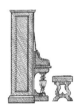

❧

The Winner

I was watching some little kids play soccer. I don't have little ones anymore, so I just watch them – and their parents. These kids were about five or six, I think. They were playing a real game – a serious game – two teams, complete with coaches, uniforms, and parents. I didn't know any of them, so I was able to enjoy the games without the distraction of being anxious about winning or losing.

I wish the parents and coaches
could have done the same.

The teams were pretty evenly matched. I will just call them Team One and Team Two. The first period passed with nobody scoring. The kids were hilarious. They were clumsy and terribly inefficient. They fell over their own feet, they stumbled over the ball, they kicked at the ball and missed it — but they didn't seem to care.

It was fun.

Winning and Losing

♦

166

In the second period, the Team One coach pulled out what must have been his first team and put in the "scrubs" — except for his best player, who now guarded the goal. The game took a dramatic turn. I guess winning is important — even when you're five years old — because the Team Two coach left his best players in, and the Team One scrubs were no match for them. They swarmed around the little guy who was now the Team One goalie. For a little kid, he was an outstanding athlete, but he was no match for three or four boys who were also very good. Team Two began to score.

He gave it everything he had, recklessly throwing his body in front of incoming balls, trying to stop them.

Team Two scored two goals in quick succession.

It infuriated the young boy. He became a raging maniac — shouting, running, diving. With all the stamina he could muster, he covered the boy who now had the ball, but that boy kicked it to another boy twenty feet away, and by the time he repositioned himself — it was too late —

they scored a third goal.

I soon learned who his parents were. They were nice, decent-looking people. I could tell that his dad had just come from the office — he still had his suit and tie on. They yelled encouragement to their son. I became totally absorbed — watching the boy on the field and his parents on the sidelines.

After the third goal, the little kid changed. He could see it was no use. He couldn't stop them, and he became frustrated. He didn't quit, but he became quietly desperate —

futility was written all over him.

His father changed too. He had been urging his son to try harder — yelling advice and encouragement. But then he changed. He became anxious. He tried to say that it was okay if they scored — he encouraged him to hang in there — he grieved for the pain in his son.

After the fourth goal, I knew what was going to happen. I have seen it before. *He needed help so badly, and there was none.* He retrieved the ball from the net and handed it to the referee —

and then he cried.

He just stood there, while huge tears rolled down both cheeks. He went to his knees. He hated crying, but what else can you do when you're all alone and there's no help? He put his fists to his eyes – his grief and frustration were so great – and he cried the tears of the helpless and brokenhearted.

When the boy went to his knees, I saw the father start onto the field. His wife clutched his arm and said, "Jim, don't. You'll embarrass him." But he tore loose from her and ran right out onto the field. He wasn't supposed to – the game was still in progress. Suit, tie, dress shoes, and all – he charged onto the field, and he picked up his son – so everybody would know he was his boy – and he hugged him and held him and cried with him.

I've never been so proud of a man in my life.

He carried him off the field, and when he got close to the sidelines I heard him say, "Scotty, I'm so proud of you. You were great out there. I wanted everybody to know that you were my son."

"Daddy," the boy sobbed, "I couldn't stop them – I did everything you told me. I tried, Daddy, I tried and tried, and they scored on me."

"Scotty, it doesn't matter how many times they score on you. You're my son, and I'm proud of you. I want you to go back and play right now. *You can't stay out of the game,* and *you're going to get scored on again,* but it *doesn't matter to us.* Go on, now."

It made a difference – I could tell it did. When you're all alone and you're getting scored on and you can't stop them – it means a lot to know that it doesn't matter to those who love you. The little guy ran back on to the field – and they scored two more times –

but it was okay.

Remember, parents – you *can't* keep your kids from getting scored on – you *can't* stop the pain – and you *can't* keep your children out of the game. You *can* let them know that you love them – that they don't have to win to get your approval – that you're proud of them in spite of the mistakes they make – and that you get "scored on" too. It makes a difference.

I get scored on every day. I try so hard. I throw my body recklessly in every direction. I fume and rage. I struggle with temptation and sin with every ounce of my being – and Satan laughs – and he scores again. And the tears come, and I go to my knees – sinful, convicted, helpless, and alone. And my Father – my heavenly Father – the God of the universe – rushes right out on the field – right in front of the whole crowd – the whole jeering, laughing world – and He picks me up, and He hugs me, and He says, "John, I'm so proud of you. You were great out there. I wanted everybody here to know that you were My son, and because I control the outcome of this game, I declare you –

the Winner."

The Price of Victory

It was Friday night, and it was late. The field house was empty – except for us, of course. We came because *it was our last chance.* One last game – just for old time's sake. We were moving. At least I was. We had played basketball so often here that we had memorized the scratches in the glass backboard and the grooves in the parquet floors. Summer, winter – seasons did not matter to us –

it was year-round basketball.

I had been playing with the boys since they were big enough to throw the ball high enough to score. Sometimes we just practiced – sometimes I played both of them – sometimes we played with others – most of the time, we played one-on-one. I always let them shoot, encouraged them, and coaxed them. I could have blocked their shots easily. When they were small, I let them score, gave them every possible advantage. At first it was no con-test, and it was fun –

we didn't even keep score.

When the oldest boy was in junior high, it began to get a little compet-itive. Between the two of them, they could push me if I relaxed too much. The older boy would get angry with the younger one when he messed up – it wasn't quite as much fun, but still fun –

but now we kept score.

The years passed, all too quickly – the older boy was a high school senior and the younger, a freshman. Now, it was all-out war. I really had to work to beat both of them – elbowing, shoving, using superior height, weight, and experience – and even then, sometimes they won. There was much arguing over lane violations, offensive fouls, who touched the ball last before it went out of bounds – and nobody encouraged anybody. The loser sulked all the way home, and it wasn't fun anymore.

Now, *only the score* was important.

The oldest boy went away to college. I was relieved. I only had to play one of them, and he was much less aggressive than his brother. The games

were slower, we didn't push and foul each other so much, and it was fun again – for a while. Then, he began to grow. When he was a junior, he was as tall as I – but still not too aggressive. When he was a senior, he was taller and becoming very strong. He could outjump me, his shooting touch was much improved, and his determination showed marked changes. The games were very close, and the arguing came back. The fun disappeared – except for winning –

and that can be very unrewarding.

He went to college where his older brother was, but we moved there. For three years we played together, separately, with others, but mostly –

one-on-one.

Tonight was the first time that it was really obvious. I was working my head off, sweat running from every pore, legs trembling from hustling loose balls – giving it everything I had. He was cruising, he was letting me shoot, giving me rebounds, keeping me in the game, trying to keep the score close –

he was carrying *me!*

Once again – it was no contest. The cycle was complete, and the fun came back –

I was enjoying myself.

God forgive me for taking the fun out of it, for purchasing my victories at the expense of their losses and achieving my satisfaction at the price of their agony. Help them to realize early what I have learned too late – that the pleasure must be

in the playing,
in being together –
that winning and losing
often destroy the best
that life has to offer.

Run, Tami, Run

While I was living in Lubbock, Texas, a dear friend who lived in Dallas called to ask if I could pick up his wife from the airport. His daughter was a very talented runner and was to run in the regional cross-country championships, which were being held in Lubbock that year. I was delighted to do it, and so I found myself on Saturday morning witnessing the Texas Regional Cross-Country Races at Mae Simmons Park. I was there *providentially,* having had no plans or even thoughts about going until my friend called. I witnessed something there – a wonderful, moving thing – a thing of beauty worth telling and retelling.

It was a marvelously bright, clear, cool morning, and hundreds of spectators had gathered on the hillsides to watch. They were mostly parents and family members who had traveled many miles – in some cases, hundreds of miles – to watch just one race. I had no child running, and so I often found myself watching those who did. Their faces were intent, their eyes always picking out the only runner they were interested in; and often, when the runners were far away and could not hear their shouts of encouragement, still their lips would move, mouthing the precious, familiar names – and *one other word.* Sometimes they would say the names softly, as if for no ears but their own, yet audibly – just because they loved to hear the sound.

"Run, Jimmy," they whispered urgently.

"Run, Tracy. Run."

The cross-country race is two miles for girls, three for boys. It is a grueling, physically and mentally exhausting run over hills and rough terrain. There were ten races that morning, beginning with class 1A boys and girls and ending with class 5A boys and girls. Each race had from eighty to one hundred twenty competitors. The course ended where it began, but at times the runners were nearly a half-mile away.

As the class 5A girls race came to a close, I watched a forty-plus-year-old mother – wearing patent leather shoes and a skirt and carrying a purse – run the last hundred yards beside her daughter. She saw no other runners. As she ran awkwardly, stumbling – her long dark hair coming undone and streaming out behind her – giving no thought to the spectacle she made – she cried, *"Run,* Tami, *run! Run,* Tami, *run!"* There were hundreds of people crowding in, shouting and screaming, but this mother was determined to be heard. *"Run,* Tami, *run! Run,* Tami, *run,"* she pleaded. The girl had no chance

to win, and the voice of her mother, whose heart was bursting with exertion and emotion, was not urging her to win.

She was urging her to finish.

The girl was in trouble. Her muscles were cramping; her breath came in ragged gasps; her stride was broken – she was in the last stages of weariness – just before collapse. But when she heard her mother's voice, a marvelous transformation took place. She straightened, she found her balance, her bearing, her rhythm – and *she finished*. She crossed the finish line, turned, and collapsed into the arms of her mother.

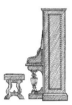

They fell down together on the grass, and they cried, and then they laughed. They were having the best time together, like there was no one else in the world but them. "God," I thought, "that is beautiful. Thank you for letting me see that."

As I drove away from Mae Simmons Park, I couldn't get it off my mind. A whole morning of outstanding performances had merged into a single happening. I thought of my own children and of a race they are running – a different and far more important race. A race that requires even greater stamina, courage, and character. I am a spectator in that race also. I have helped them train; I have pleaded – instructed – threatened – punished – prayed – praised – laughed – and cried. I have even tried to familiarize them with the course. But now the gun is up and their race has begun, and I am a *spectator*. My heart is bursting –

I see no other runners.

Sometimes their course takes them far from me, and yet I whisper, *"Run, children, run."* They do not hear, but there is One who does. Occasionally, they grow weary, because the race is long and demands such sacrifice. They witness hypocrisy, and there are many voices that call to them to quit this foolish race, telling them they cannot possibly win. They lose sight of their goal, and they falter and stumble – and I cry,

"Run, children, run – O God – please run."

And then they come to the last hundred yards – how I long to be there, to run beside them, *"Run, Lincoln; run, Debbie; run, Brendan; run, Kristen."* What if I am gone and there is no one to whisper, to shout *"Run"* in their ears? What if Satan convinces them that they are not going to win? What if his great lie – that you must beat the others – causes them to allow defeat to settle over them? What if they lose sight of the great truth – that in this race, it is *finishing* that is the victory. That is why our Lord Jesus said at the last,

"It is finished."

And that is why the great apostle Paul said,

"I have *finished* my course."

Oh God, hear my prayer. If they cannot hear my voice, if I must watch from beyond this arena – dear Lord Jesus, as you have run beside me so often – please run beside them and strengthen their knees that they might finish. And dear God, when they cross that eternal finish line, may I be there to embrace them and welcome them home. May we cry and laugh and spend eternity praising the grace by which we were given this victory.

"Run, Tami – run."

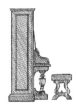

Winning
and
Losing

♦

Obedience

Obedience is
our first learned
relationship. Love
comes *after* obedience
– even as a *result* of it.

Obedience

> "Children, *obey* your parents
> in the Lord,
> for this is right.
> 'Honor your father and mother' –
> this is the first commandment with promise:
> 'so that it may be well with you
> and you may live long on the earth.' "
> —Ephesians 6:1–3 NRSV

The first duty of parents is to teach obedience. Some might question that – saying that *loving* your children is first. My response would be that loving is not a *duty* and that loving your children and teaching obedience are inseparable. Most of our problems in both areas can be traced to our attempts to treat them separately. The Bible never instructs parents to love their children, but it does instruct them – many times –

to teach obedience.

It is very important that you notice the word *teach* – because many parents only *enforce* or *demand* or *impose* obedience – and that can be done, sometimes it is even necessary – but enforcing and imposing are only tools in the teaching process.

Obedience is our first *learned* relationship. Love comes *after* obedience – even as a *result* of it. Small children know nothing of love. The apostle John says, "We love *because* He first loved us" – which means that love doesn't come first in our relationship with God, either; it is the result of our *obedience* to God, and that obedience leads to understanding His love. Small children love only themselves, and they think their wants are more important

179

than anybody else's. It's not their fault; it's simply the way of things. An infant is not concerned with his parent's finances, their rest, their schedule, their health, or their mental condition – an infant is concerned with only one thing –

its own comfort.

Obedience

♦

Until obedience is learned, no other lesson can be learned. Teaching obedience begins soon after birth. Parents who wait until their children are five or six to begin obedience training are simply courting disaster. By that age, the principle – the basic attitude of obedience – must be deeply planted. If it is not, the next few years will be increasingly filled with pain and conflict – at home – at school – in the community.

The kind of obedience we're talking about is not grudging submission to a person who has the power to impose sanctions against you. It is not the foot-dragging, sullen, resentful acquiescence of a subject to a tyrant. The obedience that God teaches – and that He expects us to both learn and teach our children – is a willing, even happy, relinquishing of our individual will to a loving wisdom that is recognized as vastly superior to our own and as always acting in our best interests.

Obedience is a *process*. The finished product is the result of a long and difficult journey. Obedience is not taught in a day – it does not result from a lesson or a hundred lessons. It comes in stages and in years.

Children have totally different personalities. Some bend quickly and easily – even passively – and some are stubbornly rebellious. Teaching techniques must be constantly adjusted to accommodate the personality of the child.

My sister and I are perfect examples of the extremes of personality. A sharply spoken reprimand from my parents absolutely crushed my sister – the slightest indication of displeasure or disappointment would reduce her to tears – to penitence – and to an immediate change in behavior. She really *wanted* to please, and she took pleasure in doing so.

Words meant almost nothing to me – they glanced off me like bullets off of Superman. I was impervious to spoken instruction. It was the old "in one ear, out the other" with me – nothing seemed to stick in between. My parents pleaded, reasoned, and threatened.

Only one thing got my attention – pain.

I am very sorry to say it – but it was true. What *I* wanted to do took precedence over all other considerations. Even when I obeyed, it was because my parents' plans agreed with my own. I took little pleasure in *pleasing others,* except when doing so *pleased me.* My choices concerning obedience were a carefully measured balance between the joy I would get from doing what I wanted and the pain I would suffer if I disobeyed.

My parents hated to give whippings – but since they were the only remedy to my affliction of disobedience – they took them seriously. Their theory was that one real good one had a more lasting effect than a dozen half-hearted ones. I always knew exactly why I was receiving a whipping, and although I dreaded them exceedingly and would promise absolutely anything to avoid one – I do not ever remember receiving one that I thought unjust. I never held it against them – never ran away from home, never even entertained the notion. I liked my home – thought it was the greatest place in the world – and couldn't conceive that anybody might have a better one.

I should explain that those were my *overall* feelings. I do not at all mean that I never had immediate or incidental resentments. Parents have to learn that children recover very quickly from punishment. That's why they repeat the unacceptable behavior so quickly after being punished for it. How many totally exasperated parents find themselves shouting, "I just punished you for this yesterday, and two days before that, and last week – when are you going to learn not to do this?"

The gymnastics that parents go through – orally, mentally, and physically – trying to avoid having to administer corporal punishment are much more stressful on both them and the child than simply doing it. Why do parents punish themselves and lose their credibility in this way? Corporal punishment is a proven method – and *properly administered,* it works. It leaves no lasting scars or irreparable damage, and most importantly –

it has the divine stamp of approval.

Most parents sort of work their way up to it – like two junior high boys trying to work up a fight. Boys have to *talk* for several days, rumors must be spread, insults have to be traded, boasts must be made about the outcome, a crowd of supporters must be present, there has to be a great deal of pushing and shoving, and of course they must make sure that there are adults in the area to break it up before anybody gets hurt. When they finally get around to trading a few half-hearted blows,

the fight itself is anticlimactic –
and so is the spanking.

Parents begin working themselves up to a spanking about the same way. They have to talk about it, and threats have to be made –

"If you do that seven more times, I'll spank you."

"Didn't I tell you that if you did that I'd spank you?"

"Did you hear me tell you that I'd spank you?"

"How many times do I have to tell you that I'll spank you for that?"

"Do you want me to spank you?"

These *threats* mean that the parent has absolutely no intention of doing any spanking at all – and the child knows that. Barking dogs do not bite – so the game goes on, and the child establishes his superiority by conforming just enough to keep the string of threats going without any action occurring.

And parents wonder why they get no respect.

The method that seems most in vogue today is the counting method. I see it quite often, and as a comedy routine it's hilarious – as a parenting method it's ludicrous. This is how it goes:

Step 1: Father and friend are standing in backyard visiting – child wanders off toward the street. The father is "on duty," so he says, "Don't go toward the street, David."

Step 2: The child takes a few more steps. The father repeats warning: "David, I said don't go toward the street. You need to come back this way." Child stops but does not return.

Step 3: The father repeats instructions – a little louder, "David, don't go toward the street. Come back toward Daddy." He returns to the conversation. The child stands and stares at his father.

Step 4: The child takes a few tentative steps toward the street and stops to make sure his father is looking. Father raises voice again, "David, did you hear what Daddy said?" Obviously, the child is not deaf, because he stops – but does not return. The battle intensity increases noticeably because the father is now under pressure because of the friend. "David, get back here this minute!"

Step 5: Child stands and stares, then sits down. Father starts counting, "One! Two!" The first two numbers come very fast, then the father realizes that he hasn't established the rules for the game, i.e., when the count ends, what happens. "David, if you're not back here before I reach five, I'll spank you." Of course he starts the count over with "one," which takes the pressure off.

Step 6: Child sits and stares: "Two! Three!" A pause – "I mean it, David." The father is pleading now; he may actually have to do something. He starts again at "Two" – long pause, "Three" – even longer pause, and no response. "Four." The father is sweating. The child looks at his father to see how serious he is and realizes his dad is in a bind. He knows he's already won the contest – he has clearly established his superiority – so he takes three steps in his father's direction. Now he has established a new basis for continuing the game. He's having the time of his life playing the national pastime – *Parent Baiting*. The game is played in homes, supermarkets, parks, and automobiles millions of times every day, much to the amusement and satisfaction of children.

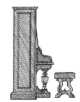

Obedience

The whole idea behind genuine obedience is that

it is not *incidental*
but *attitudinal*.

◆

I mean that the objective is not obedience to specific commands that parents teach, it is an *attitude* of obedience and respect for authority that will carry them through life. Teaching obedience is done by consistently demanding it and demonstrating it: *demonstrating* it by showing that they, too, live under authority, that they obey the rules – civil, social, and spiritual – and *demanding* it by enforcing obedience over an extended period of time until it becomes a part of the child's mental framework – not something associated only with a specific instruction.

I must not leave this critical area of instruction without adding this note. I do not remember exactly when – but somewhere about my twelfth or thirteenth year – my father very purposefully and carefully explained to me that he was never going to whip me again. He said that our relationship had to move to a higher level, a level of conscious reflection and reasoned response. What he was saying was that it was time for me to be motivated by something deeper than pain. I believe he was absolutely right.

The first step in our relationship with God is a *recognition of authority* that leads to obedience. That is the lesson that Adam and Eve did not grasp – if they had, all would be different. The history of Israel – of mankind – is a history of disobedience and the consequences of that disobedience. No other aspect of our relationship – to parents, to society, or to God – can be developed without first learning

to obey.

As a parent, a preacher, a counselor, a teacher, a coach, and a friend – I solemnly warn you. *There is no substitute for obedience,* and obedience is only learned *in one way.*

> "Though he was a Son,
> yet learned [he] *obedience*
> by the things that he *suffered.*"
> —Hebrews 5:8 ASV

Obedience

♦

Wet Feet

One of my *besetting sins* as a youngster was getting my feet wet. If I had been raised in Arizona, this would not have been such a problem, because I wouldn't have been able to find enough water to get my feet wet. But I was raised in Michigan – "The Great Lake State" – and water was everywhere. I was a child of the ditches, ponds, and streams. Wherever there were snakes, tadpoles, frogs, crayfish, or minnows, I was never far away. We did not wear boots in those days, we wore *galoshes*. Oh my goodness, they don't make galoshes anymore, do they? You don't even know what galoshes are, do you? They were black, rubber boots – calf high – that you put your whole shoe down inside of and then buckled up. Actually, my problem with wet feet was not my fault at all. The problem was that the people who made galoshes didn't understand boys very well. Consequently, they never built them tall enough or with the fronts higher than the backs so that when your leg tilted forward, the water wouldn't run in.

My mother soon grew weary of my coming home with wet feet and started whipping me on each occasion. Not meeting with any significant success, she soon pressured my father into this plot against me, and he whipped me also. I am ashamed to admit that

I was a very slow child.

I'm sure I had a "learning disability" – it's just that we used to call it "stubbornness" – and receiving two whippings per occasion only slowed me down a very little. You may wonder why having wet feet constituted such a serious problem. A major part of it was economics. The water ruined the inside of my galoshes and caused my shoes to decay. Galoshes and shoes cost money – money was very scarce – and besides, it was wasteful,

and to waste was ungodly.

You must understand that I did not *mean* to get my feet wet. It was just that whatever I was trying to catch inevitably got into water that was slightly higher than my galoshes. When I felt that icy trickle and the creeping wetness in my socks, I was absolutely sick – I knew what awaited me. When I got home, I would walk stiff legged – on my heels – so my shoes wouldn't "squish," but my mother would always notice my peculiar gait.

She would say, "John, I want you to come here."

I came.

"Yes, ma'am."

"Now, I want you to put your weight on your heels."

"Yes, ma'am."

"Now, rock forward on your toes."

"Yes, ma'am." The telltale squish was devastating.

"Do you have wet feet, John?"

"Yes, ma'am, but it isn't exactly my fault!"

"Not your fault? Did someone pour water down your pants legs and fill up your boots when you weren't looking?" There wasn't much potential in that excuse.

"No, ma'am, not exactly."

"Was there a cloudburst on the way home that filled your boots up?"

I thought about that one for a minute, but it occurred to me that if I said "Yes, that was it," she might ask me why it hadn't rained at the house.

"No, ma'am," was my mournful answer.

"Did someone push you in the ditch?" There was a little hope here.

"No, ma'am, not exactly."

"Not exactly? Or not at all?" It was no use.

"Not at all."

"Did anyone else get their feet wet on the way home?"

"I think Freddy Peterson got his a little wet."

"Well, I'll just call his mother right now and get to the bottom of this."

"Come to think of it, I believe that was last Tuesday."

"Then I assume that you were chasing something, and you got into water that was higher than your boots."

"Yes, ma'am."

"You know what this means?"

"Yes, ma'am."

"Say it."

"It means that if I ever get my feet wet again, you'll whip me."

"John, we've been over this before – say what it means!"

"You're going to whip me because I got my feet wet again, and you're going to whip me every time it happens until I quit getting my feet wet."

"Go cut me a branch off the apple tree by the chicken coop, and make it a good one. If it breaks, I'll cut one myself."

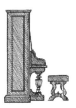

It was whipping time again. You must understand that I hated whippings – I dreaded them. You must not think that by whipping I mean some quiver-lipped, weak-kneed, half-hearted, apologetic, backhanded swat on the rear. No sir! I mean a pull your pants down, bend over that chair, knotty apple-tree branch, down to business, bottom-buster that raised quarter-inch welts and motivated one toward sobriety and repentance with loud cries and tears. I mean a *whipping!* I always solemnly promised myself that I would

never get my feet wet again.

I don't know how long this went on. My mother vowed that it lasted three years, resulted in two hundred-odd whippings, and ruined two fine apple trees.

I always thought that was an exaggeration.

My father grew weary of this merry-go-round. On one occasion, before he whipped me, he expressed this with some heat. "I'm getting sick and tired of whipping you for wet feet," he said.

That was the best news I'd had in some time,

since it was beginning to tell on me as well. I interpreted his statement to mean he was going to quit. It just goes to show how mistaken a person can be – because he proceeded to give me a whipping that made all the others pale into insignificance. He was in a considerable passion when he started, and it seemed that the longer it lasted, the more involved he became. When he finished, I hurt too much to even cry – the only time I can remember – but I promise you that he had my attention. It worked.

I stopped getting my feet wet.

Parents who fail to teach their children that unacceptable behavior has consistent and painful consequences are failing to prepare them for the real world and, even more importantly, *for a right relationship with God.* Sometimes parents need to take a page out of God's Book and

get serious with their children.

He Who Spares the Rod

The play "The Miracle Worker" is the story of the life of Helen Keller – a blind, deaf, and speechless girl who ultimately becomes an accomplished author and public speaker. It is also the story of Anne Sullivan, who helped Helen Keller become a legend in the area of overcoming handicaps.

Because of her physical liabilities, Helen is badly spoiled by her misguided and indulgent parents. She becomes an intolerable nuisance – a useless burden to her family and to herself. When Anne Sullivan is hired to train and teach Helen, she meets with peevish, sullen rebellion. When Anne attempts to discipline Helen by imposing restrictions and punishing unacceptable behavior, Helen's parents rush to defend their daughter. The major turning point in Helen's life is when Anne Sullivan confronts Helen's parents with this ultimatum:

"Helen must first learn to *obey* me –
until she does, I can teach her nothing."

The same lesson is applicable to so many areas of our lives. As a public school teacher, I learned quickly that it was more important for students to *obey* me than to *like* me. Parents left their children with me to teach them – and many of them, like Helen Keller's parents, had already rendered them unsuitable for any kind of learning, because they had not taught them the first lesson – the preschool lesson that comes before the association of letters and sounds –

the lesson of *obedience.*

A few months ago I was trying to make my way through the Atlanta Airport. My schedule was tight, not critical, but I had no time to waste. At one point I came to an impasse in the walkway – an absolute bottleneck. After much maneuvering, I finally arrived at the point of obstruction. A youngster of about eight or nine had parked his suitcase, with himself on top of it, and refused to go farther. If you had taken a measuring tape and determined the exact width of the aisle, divided it in two on a calculator that would take it to the seventeenth decimal point, you could not have found the exact center with any more precision. His mother, teary eyed and embarrassed, had also parked her belongings and was on her knees in front of him, pleading with him to move.

I have no idea what caused him to balk. I did learn that his name was Danny, but I listened to his mother grovel and beg and apologize and promise and reason with him until I was absolutely sick. And while she pleaded, the traffic stacked up behind them on every side.

A rather large man, wearing a western hat and cowboy boots, offered with some degree of *enthusiasm* to move him for her, but she would not allow him to be *forced* because it would *upset him* too much. "Force," the man said with two very descriptive expletives. "Lady, I'm not going to use force; I'm going to boot his fanny all the way to the end of the runway, and he can sit there as long as he wants!" But Danny didn't care about other people or his mother or plane schedules – or anything else but Danny. He was enjoying his rule as –

king for a day.

I felt sorry for the mother. She was pitiful. She was very smartly dressed, her hair was beautifully done, and I assume that her makeup had been as flawless as the rest of her appearance – now it was all over her face. I felt sorry for the people who were inconvenienced; I felt sorry for myself – because the incident soured my stomach and for several hours thereafter ruined an otherwise pleasurable trip; I felt sorry for Danny's school teachers – for his future wife – even for his future children; and I even felt sorry for Danny, because

I know what's in store for him.

Danny faces a lifetime of frustration, disappointment, and disillusionment. The world will soon stop bowing to his whims. There will be toys too large for his mother's purse – there will be laws that must be obeyed – and Danny will learn the lesson of obedience in a very cruel world, and Danny will suffer, and he will bring suffering

to all around him.

Danny could have learned obedience in a loving, caring atmosphere, and he could have learned it in areas of little consequence, but his parents chose to spare him and themselves that pain, and so now he will learn in a very tough school, and both he and his parents will suffer for their neglect.

If I could have asked this mother where it all began, I'm sure she would have had no idea – but I could have told her. It began with Danny in his high chair, throwing his toys on the floor and gleefully watching his mother retrieve them time after time like a faithful puppy. It began with her reading about interfering with a child's *independence* – that somehow a child

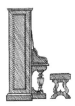

Obedience

♦

189

would *naturally* see the "reasonableness" of obedience. It began before he could walk, when he reached for something and she said "no," and then she said "no" again and again – but "no" didn't mean anything. It began when he was a toddler and his mother told him to pick up his toys – but he preferred not to – so *she* picked them up, and *she has been picking up his toys ever since.* And now, here she was on her knees in the aisle of the Atlanta airport, begging her son to move –

and she didn't know why.

God says:
"He who spares the rod
hates his son.
But he who loves him
disciplines him diligently."
—Proverbs 13:24 NASB

Who do we have our confidence in – twentieth-century psychologists who have been studying behavior for twenty years and write books about "behavior modification" – people who either have no children or whose children are woeful examples of their parents' misguided philosophy – or do we have confidence in the God who created us and who has left timeless instructions for us to follow?

Discipline

"Those who spare the rod hate their children,
but those who love them
are diligent to discipline them."
—Proverbs 13:24 NRSV

My cousin Daniel was the youngest of five children. He was raised in a house that closely resembled a cross between a three-ring circus and a Salvation Army Center. We went there often, because his mother was my mother's youngest sister, and my mother genuinely tried to help her. My aunt should never have had children. She was a pleasant woman – quick to laugh or cry, and I liked her very much – but she had no discipline. She had none for herself and none for her family – even I could see that. My uncle was a fine, hard-working man, but as a father –

he was a total failure.

I never ceased to be amazed at the absolute chaos that characterized their home. Meals were never scheduled, laundry, at all stages of going and coming, lay everywhere, the window screens were loose or torn, the shades wouldn't pull, and there always seemed to be a certain feeling of impending disaster hanging in the atmosphere. The kids knew they could get away with anything. When they committed some major infraction and my aunt got stirred up, she would grab a fly swatter and begin to chase them. Around the dining room table they would go, jumping chairs, knocking over lamps, with my aunt in hot pursuit, waving her fly swatter. Then she would get tired and she could see how ridiculous she was, and it tickled her. She would collapse in a chair, all in a heap, and she would laugh until she cried.

That was discipline at my aunt's house.

Danny and I were pretty close for a while. He was a handsome boy, with a pleasant personality. He was never disciplined at home, and his parents gave him every conceivable gift – things they simply could not afford. He had a flaming temper, and he was quick to lie. He was often in trouble – first in the neighborhood, then at school, and finally with the authorities. My aunt and uncle always took his side. The teachers were all against him. The neighbors just didn't like him and accused him unjustly. They excused and defended him against all accusations, against all reason –

even *against the facts.*

When Danny's problems began to get serious, and other problems in his home occurred simultaneously, he came to stay with us. I believe my aunt and uncle realized that they had lost all control and that Daniel had no respect for them. They hoped that with the "heavier hand" of my father, Danny would do better. He did. He honestly improved some, but just when it seemed he might really make some lasting changes, he would appeal to his folks, and they would relent and let him come back home.

It was never long until he was in trouble again.

My father was very kind to him – and very understanding too – but he punished him severely for recalcitrance. On one occasion, the last time he came to us, he took some money from my mother's purse. I saw him do it and warned him, but he was accustomed to doing it at home with no fear of reprisal. We were in the living room when my father confronted him. He lied and said he hadn't done it. My father told him that he was going to give him one more chance to be a man and face up to his guilt, but Danny was too steeped in his old ways, and he little understood my father.

"No," he said again, "I didn't take it."

My father told him he was going to be punished for lying and stealing. I think Danny had some notion of maybe missing supper or being confined to his room. You cannot imagine how confused he looked, when my father told him to get up and go outside with him.

"What are we going to do?" he asked.

I could have told him.

"I'm going to whip you, and you're going to be sorry," my father replied.

Danny had never been "whipped" in his life, and his lack of understanding of my father led him to an even greater mistake – he refused to get up; he sat clinging to the arms of his chair.

"Daniel" – my father's voice was dangerously quiet, and any time my father called you by your given name, it was serious – "you can either walk outside or be carried outside – chair and all. I'm getting mad, and that is not good for you."

I was terrified, and I wasn't even involved. I wanted to tell Danny that the best possible solution was to excuse himself, go to the bathroom, and cut his throat – but I knew better than to speak. They went outside – Danny walked – and my father whipped him. I could hear the whistling cracks of the switch and his cries. My whole body squirmed and ached in sympathy with his.

My father made his point with Danny, and he improved – he honestly did. Then he left again, and I didn't see him for some time. One day, I overheard my parents talking about him being sent to a juvenile detention center.

During his stay there, he ran away twice. Do you know where he went when they were hunting for him? Did he return home where he had never been punished or reproved? No! *He came to us – both times.* He came late at night. He came to the only place that had brought order to his disordered life, the only place where lines were clearly drawn and where he had been punished for crossing them.

I felt so sorry for him. He would be thin and worn, poorly dressed and scared. He was still only just a boy, and life's realities were hard on him. My father always allowed him to stay a while, and they talked much. We fed him and clothed him, but since he was a fugitive, he had to go back. He would plead with my father, vowing to change his ways, and he meant it too.

But it could not be.

Daniel suffered. He suffered for his parent's sins, and for his own as well. The Hebrew author asks us, "What son is there whom his father does not discipline?" The answer to that question is obvious – an *unloved* son. Scripture tells us plainly that God disciplines us. It is an integral part of His love. We are even told that God's discipline brings sorrow – the implication is that it may be severe in nature. God disciplines us so that "we may share His holiness." God's purpose in discipline is never to punish; the *purpose* is always to *correct* and *instruct,* and our motives must be the same. The only right *purpose* for discipline is *altered behavior.*

"Discipline your children while there is hope;
do not set your heart on their destruction."
—Proverbs 19:18 NRSV

Daisy

I had a two-hour layover in Dallas. I parked myself in an out-of-the-way corner because I had reading to do and did not wish to be disturbed. I was reading – actually rereading – *The Great Gatsby,* F. Scott Fitzgerald's magnificent description of the shallowness, extravagance, and excess of the Roaring Twenties. I was using it as a text for an American novel class I was teaching at Faulkner University. Fitzgerald's female heroine is named Daisy. How many Daisys do you know? In all of my teaching and preaching career, spanning thirty-five years and ten states, I have never met nor heard of a female named Daisy, with the exception of a ridiculous song I used to hear my mother sing – which went something like this –

"Daisy Maisie, give me your answer true.
I'm half crazy, all for the love of you.

It won't be a stylish marriage;
I can't afford a carriage.
But you'll look sweet upon the seat
Of a bicycle built for two."

Obedience

♦

194

There are no areas of the Dallas airport where a person is totally alone, but I had found one with relatively few people. There were a few scattered businessmen with the inevitable briefcase – as much a part of their dress as the dark suit, white shirt, black shoes, and loosened tie – by which they maintain their identity. On my left, about ten seats away, was a young, Oriental boy – sipping a coke and reading intently. To my right, seven or eight seats away, was a young mother with a two- or three-year-old daughter.

What follows is a blow-by-blow description of events. I became so intrigued that I actually took out my notebook and recorded them as they happened. I am often guilty of embellishment, exaggeration, and the addition of color. In this case, the actual facts

are quite sufficient.

I was reasonably well *settled in,* when the young mother noticed that her daughter had wandered farther than she was comfortable with and called her to come back to her seat. "Daisy," she cried, "come back here."

I had Fitzgerald's book right in my hand – it was incredible. I became fascinated by Daisy and her mother. The child was dressed beautifully, very ornately, with frilly and elaborate clothing, but her shoes had been removed. The mother was dressed very casually, and she had also removed her shoes. Daisy was bored, and she again began to explore the area. The first three *chases* I witnessed were simply the routine type – when Daisy wandered too far or threatened the peace of other travelers. Each chase was preceded by the mother first pleading, then coaxing, then threatening. Daisy was oblivious. Her mother might as well have been whistling the proverbial *Dixie.* Meeting no success with her threats, she would heave herself to her feet, chase Daisy down, catch her, and bring her back – kicking, struggling, and screaming.

Chase number four began when Daisy spit a piece of candy on the carpet. The mother told her to pick it up.

Daisy preferred not to
and stood glaring at her mother
in open defiance.

Eventually, the mother came and picked it up – much to Daisy's satisfaction – and asked her if she wanted another piece. After four repetitions of the question, Daisy agreed to take one, but she would not take it with her hand. She stood with her mouth wide open, like a baby bird, demanding that her mother place it in her mouth. When the mother obediently complied, Daisy bit her fingers, apparently quite hard, because her mother gasped – then screamed. As she stood, first shaking her injured fingers, then placing them in her own mouth, Daisy laughed and ran –

chase number five ensued.

Daisy's next excursion was in my direction. Out of the corner of my eye, I saw her coming. She was taking her time, whacking each intervening seat with her fist, but I was definitely the objective. She really was cute. She whacked the seat beside me and then paused, right in front of me, chubby little fist raised high in a threatening position, waiting for my response. I kept my eyes on my book, refusing to either look at her or acknowledge her presence. Daisy wasn't used to being ignored. She tapped me on the knee – I ignored her – she tapped harder and made little gurgly baby noises, demanding me to pay attention – I ignored her. She raised her foot and brought it down as hard as she could on my toe. She had no shoes on, and it didn't hurt –

but it made me mad –
and sad.

"Is she bothering you?" The mother's voice inquired.

"Yes," I said, "but not as you mean it."

She looked at me – and was about to express her bewilderment when she was interrupted by a scream. Daisy had spotted another child, some distance away, who had a small stuffed animal. With no hesitation, she had run, snatched the stuffed animal from the unsuspecting child, and had started toward her mother. Her scream of indignation was prompted when the child tried to recapture the toy. Daisy, realizing that her mother was not on her side, turned and ran down the main aisle – chase number six was in progress. The mother eventually brought her back to the area, pleading with her to surrender the animal, and finally, by sheer, physical strength, wrenched it from Daisy's death grip – damaging the toy in the process –

while Daisy screamed bloody murder.

The mother now held Daisy and paraded up and down in front of the huge plate-glass windows overlooking the plane refueling and parking area. She pointed to everything of interest she could find to distract Daisy's attention from her recent setback. She partially succeeded – to the great relief of everyone in the area. Worn out – she returned to a seat somewhat closer to me than previously. Embarrassed, apologetic, and obviously frustrated, she

Obedience

◆

said, "I just can't wait till she gets a little older, so I can begin disciplining her."

"It will soon be entirely too late," I said.

"Oh, do you think so?" she asked with interest.

"I know so," I said.

She wanted to ask something else, but she noticed that Daisy had taken one of her shoes and made off with it. "Come back here," she called, and there was genuine anger in her voice — but it didn't matter to Daisy — she had heard it before, and she knew there was nothing behind it. Chase number seven ended with Daisy throwing the shoe into the main aisle just as her mother caught her. She brought her back, plopped her in the seat beside her and said,

Obedience

"Now, don't you move."

By now many of the other travelers had vacated the area. The oriental teenager — had remained. He would sip his coke and then place it on the seat beside him as he turned pages. A few minutes passed without incident, and I returned to my book. Chase number eight occurred when the mother apparently closed her eyes for a moment and dozed off — the wandering Daisy took the unattended soft drink and made off with it. As she attempted to escape, she tripped and fell, spilling the contents, mostly on the floor, some on herself, and some on the shoes and pants of a businessman who had remained in the area.

The mother wiped off Daisy, apologized to the businessman, and tried to give the oriental boy enough money to replace the soft drink. The boy, who apparently spoke little English, was incredulous, having never, I'm sure, witnessed such behavior in his life.

Chase number nine was when Daisy ran under the restraining ropes and down the enplaning and deplaning ramp.

Eventually our plane arrived, and we began to board. I looked for Daisy and her mother and spotted them being seated in the area of my seat. I thought, "Surely God wouldn't do that to me." A two-hour flight from Dallas to Atlanta sitting next to Daisy would be enough provocation to wait for a later flight.

I was right.
God didn't do that to me.
I was two rows behind them.

Though He Was a Son

"Though he was a Son, yet [he] learned obedience
by the things which he suffered."
—Hebrews 5:8 ASV

The Porters lived about a quarter mile west of us. Their house sat way back off the road, and it was almost totally hidden by huge, old maples and elms. It was sort of a forbidding old place, and the neighborhood kids did not cross their property. Mrs. Porter was a step back in time with her flowing dresses that reached down to the ground and her bonnets and shawls. I saw her often, working in her flowers, shrubs, and garden. She was always stooped over or on her knees. I thought she didn't like me much, because

she never smiled or spoke.

My father had bought me a great present, something almost beyond value – a Buck Jones, pump action, BB gun. When he gave it to me, he was very serious, and he warned me sternly about its proper use. He gave me a specific list of birds that I could shoot – starlings, blackbirds, grackles, and sparrows. I was to kill no songbirds, no blue jays, robins, or cardinals. I was so excited about the BB gun and so anxious to get out and shoot it that I paid little attention, I fear; but when he asked if I understood, I said yes and promised to obey.

One morning I killed a blackbird (actually it was a grackle), which was sitting on the telephone wires in front of the Porters' house. I went over to inspect my prey, and that feeling of shame, which always confused and irritated me when I killed a bird, came over me. I was standing there, alone with my thoughts, when Mrs. Porter appeared. I hadn't seen her because she was hidden by her lilac bushes. When I say "appeared," you must understand that I mean that literally. One moment I was alone, the next moment she was there – not there as in thirty feet – but there, as in two feet. She absolutely scared me speechless. I thought she was a wraith, with her bonnet down over her face and her loose garments flapping in the wind.

"What did you shoot?" she demanded in a very accusing tone.

"A starling," I stammered. The bird was lying right at my feet.

Mrs. Porter lifted my face to hers by my chin and said, "You dumb boy. That's no starling, that's a grackle. I hate starlings and grackles as much as anybody – but don't you ever kill any songbirds near my place!"

"Yes, ma'am." I said –

and I meant it.

About two or three weeks went by. I was going to see my friend, Doug Bussey, who lived next door to the Porters. I had my Buck Jones with me – I never went anywhere without it. It was a pretty, sunny, June day, tailor-made for a nine-year-old boy. I was barefoot, tanned, and looking for adventure. Sitting on the telephone wire in front of the Porters', singing his heart out, was a yellow-breasted canary. There were many warning voices saying, "No!" "Don't even think about it." But there was another voice – stronger than my father's warning – stronger than Mrs. Porter's imprecations – stronger than my fear of whipping – stronger than all of the inner voices of teaching and conscience – the voice of what *I wanted to do* –

and I shot the canary.

Oh, I told myself I was just going to scare it – but I killed it deader than a hammer. I looked around quickly – certain that Mrs. Porter would descend upon me from some unseen quarter, but no one came.

I went on my way quickly,
conscience stricken,
leaving behind me the tiny,
unoffending body of a songbird.

Two days later, sitting at the supper table, with absolutely no explanation, my father told me that we were going to the Porters' that evening after supper. Even my mother was going.

We had never been to the Porters' before,
and there could be only one reason for going now.
I was terrified.

I still remember the walk to the Porters'. My father and mother walked rather rapidly, with firmness and resolution; they did not talk to me or to each other. Normally, I would have been running ahead, making side excursions, and showing off – but on this night, I slunk along behind, dreading the termination of our journey.

I remember that the Porters' house was large. The ceilings in the rooms were much higher than ours, and the things on the walls were ornate and looked expensive to my unpracticed eye. Everything looked old and fragile. With my natural propensity for breaking things, I was scared to move. The room we sat in was painfully clean and orderly. I sat in a chair much too large for me –

and I was most uncomfortable.

After the initial courtesies had passed, my father informed me that Mrs. Porter had seen me shoot the canary. Since I had broken my word to him, and since I had openly shown disrespect for Mrs. Porter, I must be punished. We were here to determine how I could best repay Mrs. Porter and demonstrate my penitence. My father was very severe in his manner, and I knew that he was deeply hurt and disappointed by my conduct. I was genuinely penitent, and began to cry – not just because I had hurt my father, but also because I knew that what was in store for me was not going to be pleasant.

Mrs. Porter got up and came to where I was sitting and stood by my chair. I guess I'd never really looked at her before – I mean, I'd never really seen her. She always looked like a large woman, but actually, she was very small. I guess it was her loose, baggy clothing that had made me think her large. She was bent and crooked, and her white hair was thin and wispy. Her face was pinched and wrinkled, but not at all unpleasant, just old. She told me she had a lot of yard work she wanted done and that after I had done some for the bird, she would pay me for the rest. But, she added, there was one other condition that absolutely must be met. I had visions of my Buck Jones broken into pieces. I was not prepared at all – neither were my folks –

for the condition she named.

A few weeks earlier, my parents had invited their church friends to our house for watermelon and singing. About sixty or seventy had come. We had sung out by the grape arbor until very late at night. We did not know it, but the Porters had heard us, and they had walked down the road and listened for some time. The final condition of my probation was that

I must sing for Mrs. Porter.

When we got home, my father and I went outside. He told me that I was to work hard for Mrs. Porter and that any report of the slightest refractory behavior on my part would lead to the most serious consequences. I begged him not to make me go to the Porters'. I even told him I would take a whipping (you simply cannot know what a concession that was), but he was absolutely implacable. To make matters worse, he told me that I was going to receive a whipping anyway – because I had broken my word. I still remember the pain in his voice as he told me what a serious sin I had committed. He explained that our total relationship was based on *trust,* and when

Obedience

♦

199

that trust was violated, we could never be sure of each other. I know I didn't understand all he said, but I understood very well that lying was serious in our family and that folks who lied, or who didn't keep their commitments, were

pretty much useless.

Obedience

♦

When I went to bed that night, still smarting from the whipping I had received, I believe I was aware of "alienation" for the first time. Oh, I didn't call it by that name – I had no name for it at all – but I knew that my father hadn't come to my room to say goodnight to me and that what I had done had separated us somehow.

For the next three weeks, except Sundays, I trooped to the Porters' at daylight, and Mrs. Porter – and occasionally Mr. Porter – and I worked in the shrubs and garden. At first the work was drudgery and the singing hard – I couldn't think of songs to sing. But gradually, one song would remind me of another, and sometimes Mrs. Porter would ask me to repeat one. After two or three days, she began to hum bits and pieces and sing a word now and then, and all in all, it wasn't too bad. Mrs. Porter would fix lunch for us, and we would talk. She would ask me all kinds of questions and tell me about herself. Sometimes lunch lasted most of the afternoon. I learned they had no children. When my time of confinement was up, we parted, but ever after we were friends, and the Porter house was no longer forbidding to me – but friendly – and I seldom passed without a smile or a "Hello, Johnny."

During the last week, my father started coming to the Porters' and waiting for me until I finished my work. Sometimes he would sing with me, and Mrs. Porter would join in, and we would have a grand time. While he waited, he would talk to Mr. Porter. We would walk home together. Sometimes he would tell me about his job (it was wartime, and he worked at the tank arsenal); sometimes we would just walk quietly. It was my father's way of saying that I was forgiven and that everything was all right now.

I was always grateful for his company.

The Hebrews author tells us in chapter two that God thought it fitting to perfect Jesus, the author of our salvation, *through suffering*. He also states in chapter five that Jesus *learned obedience* from the things He suffered. That's how I learned obedience – through the things I suffered. How tragic it is that in our society, children are raised as painlessly as possible, until those inevitable times come when we can no longer physically, financially, or emotionally shield or rescue them. Most parents either wait too long or impose suffering on their children in such a way that obedience is not what is learned – only rebellion and anger. And we wonder why our children lack self-discipline, character, sensitivity, and moral fiber.

Those things are only learned in one way.

What marvelous lessons I learned as a boy. God must have a special place in His great heart for mischievous boys who must always learn hard. I thank God daily for my father – a kind, tender, compassionate man who could be stern and strong and absolutely unbending when he thought it was called for. And I thank God for the Porters and what I learned there.

I have never –
not till this very day –
ever killed another songbird.

You see, my father not only taught me *obedience* and *forgiveness* – he taught me *piety* –

a feeling of deep respect
for the sacredness of all of God's creation.

A Broken Spirit

"Create in me a pure heart, O God,
and renew a steadfast spirit within me. . . .
The sacrifices of God are a broken spirit;
a broken and contrite heart."
—Psalm 51:10, 17 NIV

There are two things you must understand in order to get the meaning of this story. The first is very hard to believe, but it's true: when I was growing up, we had no "indoor plumbing" – consequently, we had an *outhouse*. It wasn't much of an outhouse, but it was the only one we had.

The second thing is easy to believe: I was a very stubborn and rebellious child.

Those of you who have been culturally deprived and therefore have not had the "outhouse experience," have been robbed of one of life's most interesting opportunities. Having to use an outhouse on a regular basis develops character. It seems to me that every college ought to offer a mandatory class in things like wringer washers, TVs with no remote controls, and

outhouses.

We had an outhouse. It was about thirty yards from the house and about six feet from the back of the chicken coop. It was old, gray, weathered, and large – large enough for my father to store bales of hay in it.

We took great pride in the fact that it was a "two-holer." You know, looking back, I wonder about the reason for that, because *I have no recollections of two people ever using it at the same time* – it isn't exactly a "social sitting" (pun intended). I mean, can you imagine sitting there in an old, smelly, cold, dark, damp, outhouse and having an intellectually stimulating conversation?

"Nice day."

"Yep."

"Hand me the catalog, would you?"

"Sure don't make catalogs the way they used to, do they?"

"Nope. Back when they came in black and white they were better. All that colored ink sure messes up your underwear."

"Say, do me a favor – don't use the tools and sporting goods section; I haven't read that yet."

"Okay, and my wife wants the clothing section."

Maybe the two holes were just for "bragging rights."

I hated the trip out there – especially when it was dark. In the summer, it was the mosquitoes, the swooping bats, and the eerie, drifting noises of the creatures who lived in the swamp below our house. In the winter, it was the shadowy night, the sound of the wind in the trees, the hooting owls, the cold, hard seat, and the rustling rats that lived in the hay bales – when one of them ran over my toes, it scared me so bad I didn't have to go anymore – and you have to hate that. At any time, it was that ominous, dark opening – that opening that might hold anything – spiders – wasps – or worse. When I awoke late at night and had to go, all of these factors combined to make me draw my knees up under my chin – hold it – and pray to God to please

let the sun come up.

Our house – and the outhouse – sat on a hill that overlooked the swamp, where millions of cattails grew. In late summer they ripened – and not only did they look like long, fat cigars, when properly lit they smoldered like cigars – and smelled ten times better. Some folks gathered and lit them because the smoke drove off the mosquitoes.

James and I lit them
just for the fun of it.

On one occasion we had cut hundreds of them, and we were lighting them as rapidly as possible. Some were still green, and they burned very reluctantly. This was not to be tolerated, so I suggested that we stick them down the long-necked kerosene can – that my father also stored in the outhouse – and soak them. After that, they burned spectacularly, and I thought I was very clever. Because we had few matches, we used the burning cattails to light the unlit ones.

James had just soaked one – apparently pretty thoroughly, because the excess kerosene ran down the stalk and onto his hand. As he came out of the outhouse, I was going in. My burning cattail touched his unlit one and ignited it – the flames raced down the stalk and onto his hand. His immediate reaction was to throw the cattail – and he did – right into the hay bales. The resulting conflagration was breathtaking. We stood in absolute awe, as the old, dry, weather-beaten outhouse went up in flames.

My mother came out – in a state of some excitement – and frantically tried to organize an effort to put it out. She tried to enlist James and me, but her directions were confusing, and truthfully, our efforts were less than half-hearted. Every time we went for a bucket of water – which had to be pumped by hand – we missed some of the excitement. Besides, even a child could see that it was hopeless. It was amazing how quickly the whole thing collapsed and fell – sizzling – right into the hole over which it had stood for so many years.

I wasn't sorry to see it go –

until I thought of how my father would react when he got home. I was pretty sure he wouldn't be too happy with the afternoon's activities.

When he pulled into the driveway, I was on the front porch with my mother. Normally, I would have met him at the road and raced alongside the car as he pulled up to the house – but not today.

Today, I stood behind my mother.

He knew something was wrong right off, and he knew that it involved me – because it always did. He got out of the car and said, "Well what did he do this time?" He sounded discouraged.

"He burned down the outhouse," Mom said. She just said it matter of factly, like it was something I did every day. She said it with no preliminary

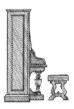

Obedience

♦

203

at all. I mean she could have said, "He hoed the garden, fed the chickens, and burned down the outhouse." She made it sound like I had deliberately set fire to it. She also forgot to say that James had actually done it, and I just happened to be there.

"What?" my father said. It wasn't the kind of "what" that means you didn't understand or hear – it was the kind of "what" that signifies amazement or disbelief.

Slowly, carefully, she repeated, "John – burned – down – the – outhouse." It was like "read my lips" – and again, she left James out.

My dad didn't say a word; he just set his lunchpail down on the front porch and walked around the corner of the house – like he wouldn't believe it until he saw it. My mother and I walked behind him. You know how sometimes you can want something to be true so badly that you begin to believe that it *is* true? Well, I wanted that outhouse to be there when we turned that corner. I wanted it so much that I thought it would be – I mean it had always been there; why shouldn't it be there now? Maybe I had just *imagined* that it had burned down; maybe God had put it back when I wasn't looking. But he hadn't. When we turned the corner –

it was definitely gone.

Dad never said a word about it. He told me to go get his lunchpail, and we went into the house. My mother explained, now, in some detail what had happened, and this time she included James – which was a great relief to me – except somehow James didn't come out looking quite as bad as he would have if I had told the story. I had not said a word. My dad said that after supper he would go up to see James's dad, Mr. MacFarland.

He didn't have to. Mr. MacFarland and James came down to our house, and the two fathers stood out close to where the outhouse had been and talked quietly for quite a while. James and I stood at a distance and waited. We knew we were going to die – we just didn't know by what method they were going to execute us. When they finished talking, they called James and me over and told us what they had decided. Our punishment would be that we would dig the hole for the new outhouse by hand, with spades. The dirt from the new hole would fill the old one. They laid out the dimensions with stakes and string.

That night my dad came to my room and talked to me.

"Why did you stick those cattails down the kerosene can?"

"To make them burn better."

"You knew you were doing wrong, didn't you?"

"You never told me not to."

"But you knew better, didn't you? You wouldn't have done it if I had been home, would you?"

"I don't know."

"Yes, you do know, and I want to hear you say that you do."

"All right. I wouldn't have done it if you had been home."

"Son, do you ever wonder why you're always in trouble?"

"It has crossed my mind."

"Until you learn to do what you know to be *right,* instead of what you *want* to do, you're going to continue to be in trouble."

"But James – "

"I don't want to hear another word about James. Not one bit of this was James' fault – isn't that right?"

"If *you* say so."

"I want *you* to say so, and we're going to stay here until you do."

"Okay, it was all my fault."

◆

He was right. He never yelled – never raised his voice. When you're right, you don't have to –

but I didn't *believe* he was right –
no, not even a little.

The next morning my dad got me up before daylight. After breakfast, James and his dad came down, and just at daylight, we began. We suffered. It is no exaggeration – we really did. We stayed at it from early morning till late evening – two boys, eight or nine years old – digging a hole, eight feet deep, four feet wide, and eight feet long. We handed up dirt in buckets when the hole was over our heads. We had no gloves, so our hands burned and blistered. The pain of just gripping a shovel was almost unbearable. Then the blisters broke and the calluses formed. I do not remember exactly, but I believe it took us two weeks.

The punishment did not make me sorry – it made me bitterly resentful. The harder and the longer I worked, the more angry I became. My injured pride and rebellious anger made me sullen and withdrawn. There was no reason I should be punished for James's stupidity. I thought my father the most heartless, unjust tyrant that ever lived. I would not speak to him unless I was forced to.

He could make me *work,*
but he couldn't make me *sorry* –
no sir –
nothing was *ever* going to make me sorry.

I'm sure my father wavered. He probably questioned his decision, but he saw it through. The night we finished, he came to my room after supper. I had gone there directly after eating to display my lack of penitence and to nurse my wrongs. He stood in the doorway. He quietly complimented me on doing a good job and staying with a very difficult assignment.

He said he was proud of me.

I was so tired, I felt so wronged, I was so angry – and I was only just a boy. My indignation finally welled up, and I began to speak – to pour out my resentment in a jumbled torrent. I told him how unfairly he had treated me, how mean and unjust he was, and I didn't care if he killed me, I was going to have my say.

My father stood quietly, his broad shoulders slightly stooped and pain written in every line of his face. I know now that he thought he had failed.

I'm not sure just what it was that broke my stubborn will. I'd like to think it was my love for my father, maybe it was something in his face – the pain, the failure – that caused me to end my tirade by rushing to him and burying my face in his shirt – I threw my arms around him and sobbed – "I'm sorry, Dad, I'm sorry" –

and I really was, you know.

It was the first experience with "brokenness" that I remember. When I went to bed, my father knelt beside me and prayed. He thanked God for changing my heart. He asked God to help him to be a better father and to help me to be a better son. His prayer made a lasting impression on me – not because it was long, but because it brought God into my life at a very important moment and in a very practical way.

There can be no spiritual or emotional growth without the experience of brokenness. Only through suffering can we develop the humility that allows us to be of value to others – to ourselves – and to God. Only then, can we begin to appreciate what He has done for us in Jesus.

You cannot successfully raise children without taking great "risks." There is no absolutely safe, guaranteed way. Those who lack the courage or the self-discipline to take risks in child raising, who always take the "safe" method, are risking the most – they risk making no lasting impressions. Sometimes, you just don't know how things are going to turn out. I admire my father's wisdom and his faith that he was doing the right thing. Some lessons will only be learned by imposing harsh punishments that last over days – sometimes weeks. Every time I moved a shovel full of dirt, I was taking a step toward a clean heart and a broken spirit.

Obedience

◆

207

"Create in me a pure heart, O God,
and renew a steadfast spirit within me. . . .
The sacrifices of God are a broken spirit;
a broken and contrite heart."
—Psalm 51:10, 17 NIV

Obedience

♦

208

NINE

Memories of
Clark Road

A good memory –
especially a memory
of childhood, of
home – is perhaps the
best education.

Memories of Clark Road

Most of the first ten years of my life were lived in about a square mile. The square mile was bounded by Eighteen Mile Road to the south, Nineteen Mile Road to the north, Rochester Road to the east, and Livernois Road to the west. I lived very close to the corner of Eighteen Mile Road and Rochester Road –

on Clark Road.

The map displayed in the first story of this chapter is a map of that neighborhood. The education I received there, in the form of *good memories,* has sustained me through the temptations, doubts, and loneliness of sixty years.

Occasionally, I come across something in my reading that speaks so forcefully, directly, and beautifully to my heart that I realize that I cannot say it better – or, as in this case, I could not say it so well – and so I bring it to you as I found it.

It is from *The Brothers Karamazov,* by Fyodor Dostoyevsky. The setting for this "sermon" is this: Alyosha, the speaker, is addressing a group of young boys – probably ten to thirteen years old. They have gathered at "Ilusha's stone," in memory of their friend Ilusha, who has just died. The stone was a favorite place of his, and it was his wish to be buried there. These boys had all been childhood enemies of Ilusha, but in the last days of his life, during his illness, they were reconciled by their teacher, Alyosha, and came to love, not only their former enemy, Ilusha – but each other.

Let me beg you to read this account slowly – let these beautiful words wash over your soul. They will bring cleansing, peace, hope, and renewed determination to live a better life. I have italicized those phrases that I most want you to notice.

> My dear children, perhaps you won't understand what I am saying to you, because I often speak very unintelligibly, but you'll remember it all the same and will agree with my words sometimes. You must know that *there is nothing higher and stronger and more wholesome and good for life in the future than some good memory, especially a memory of childhood, of home.* People talk to you a great deal about your education, but *some*

Memories of
Clark Road

♦

214

good, sacred memory, preserved from childhood, is perhaps the best education. If a man carries any such memories with him into life, he is safe to the end of his days, and *if one has only one good memory left in one's heart, even that may sometime be the means of saving us.* Perhaps we may even grow wicked later on, may be unable to refrain from a bad action, may laugh at men's tears and at those people who say as Kolya did just now, 'I want to suffer for all men,' and may even jeer spitefully at such people. But however bad we may become – which God forbid – yet, when we recall how we buried Ilusha, how we loved him in his last days, and how we have been talking like friends all together, at his stone, the cruelest and most mocking of us – if we do become so – will not dare to laugh inwardly at having been kind and good at this moment! What's more, *perhaps, that one memory may keep him from great evil* and he will reflect and say, 'Yes, I was good and brave and honest then.' Let him laugh to himself, that's no matter, a man often laughs at what's good and kind, that's only from thoughtlessness. But I assure you, boys, that as he laughs he will say at once in his heart, 'No, I do wrong to laugh, for that's not a thing to laugh at.' "

The years I spent on Clark Road formed the foundation for the rest of my life. Those were the years before puberty – before girls – before sin. Not only were they the most happy, carefree, and innocent years of my life, it was during that time that I developed a fixed sense of identity – of who I was – of what it meant to be a Smith and a Christian. I learned that being a Smith meant that I always told the truth, worked hard, went to church every time the doors were open –

and never wasted anything.

I learned that fear is often a valid motivation for action and that God provides the light of hope – even in the darkest tunnel. Those memories and that identity have never left me.

Children who grow up with a consciousness of who they are – based upon their understanding of the ongoing history that connects the past with the future – will live more purposefully, thoughtfully, and prayerfully. They will be less selfish and will develop a wider consciousness and perspective of life and their places in society.

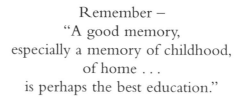

Remember –
"A good memory,
especially a memory of childhood,
of home . . .
is perhaps the best education."

Where Does the Stuff Go?

To go to school, I walked down Clark Road to Rochester Road. (I say *down* because Clark Road sloped uphill from Rochester Road to my house.) Anyway, I walked down Clark Road to Rochester Road, turned south about three hundred yards to Eighteen Mile Road, turned east about one mile to John R. Road and there it was, Colerain School – three rooms, eight grades – where the finest minds of the century were honed to a razor sharp edge – well –

perhaps something slightly less than that.

Walking back and forth to school was a much anticipated event. In fact, I enjoyed it so much that school itself was anticlimactic. Few days passed without incident, and the education I received from it has outlasted my classroom experiences.

The three hundred yards between Clark Road and Eighteen Mile Road were particularly gratifying because of the swamp. Rochester Road was the east boundary of the swamp, and the edge of the road was lined with cattails and marsh grass. Of course, swamp creatures collected there, especially during the dry season – snakes, turtles, crayfish, muskrats, frogs, and leeches. On the way to school, my friends and I were always poking around, pulling the

215

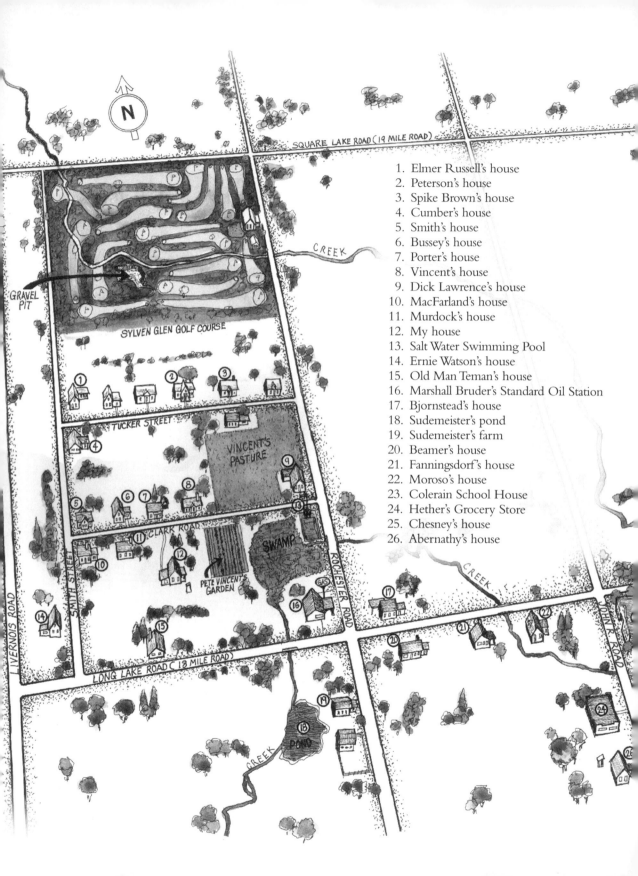

1. Elmer Russell's house
2. Peterson's house
3. Spike Brown's house
4. Cumber's house
5. Smith's house
6. Bussey's house
7. Porter's house
8. Vincent's house
9. Dick Lawrence's house
10. MacFarland's house
11. Murdock's house
12. My house
13. Salt Water Swimming Pool
14. Ernie Watson's house
15. Old Man Teman's house
16. Marshall Bruder's Standard Oil Station
17. Bjornstead's house
18. Sudemeister's pond
19. Sudemeister's farm
20. Beamer's house
21. Fanningsdorf's house
22. Moroso's house
23. Colerain School House
24. Hether's Grocery Store
25. Chesney's house
26. Abernathy's house

reeds apart, prying into every opening, looking for something to catch – or throw rocks at.

About halfway between Clark Road and Eighteen Mile Road was a very large culvert, which ran under Rochester Road and drained off the excess water from the swamp. During hard rains, it would be half-filled with rushing water, but sometimes it was totally dry. The culvert must have been four or five feet in diameter, and we walked through it and played in it often. When big trucks passed over us, it trembled and echoed, which was deliciously exciting, and we thought we were very daring.

On our way to school one Monday morning in late spring – after a weekend of very heavy rainfall – we were astounded to find that the water in the swamp was almost level with Rochester Road – the culvert was totally submerged – and where it normally could be seen, there was now a gigantic whirlpool! It was fascinating. We stood there in unbelief. We had never seen such a thing. We began to throw things into it – sticks and other debris that had washed up to the edge of the water. Round and round they went – ever increasing in speed, narrowing the circle, drawn inevitably into that central vortex, which consumed them and took them from sight.

One of the boys – Freddie Peterson, I think – caught a small frog and threw it in. We watched in dumb amazement as the frog struggled frantically to break out of the sucking grip of the whirlpool, but he didn't have a chance. He made some headway at first, but he grew tired. Finally, exhausted, he succumbed, and he, too, disappeared from sight.

It never occurred to any of us that the whirlpool was caused by the culvert. You must understand that. We couldn't see it, and we did not connect the two things. It was a great mystery.

"Where does the stuff go?"

we asked ourselves. Into what horrible, bottomless pit did it ultimately come to spend a dark eternity?

We really hated to leave, and we were all late to school that day. As I sat in class, my mind kept returning to the whirlpool; it bothered me all day.

"Where does the stuff go?" I wondered.

I don't know when or how it occurred to me. I believe that somehow in thinking about the whirlpool, my imagination created a visual image of the area, and in that image I saw the whole scene – like from a helicopter – and *in the larger picture* I could see the other side of Rochester Road, the culvert opening, and the creek that was formed by the swamp water.

Memories
of Clark
Road

♦

217

"Of course," I thought —
"the stuff doesn't go *down* at all —
it comes out on the other side —
the side we never walk on!"

I was so happy — so excited — I couldn't wait to test my theory on the way home.

I did it very dramatically. I found an old chunk of wood laying beside the road and carried it with me. I waited until we got to the whirlpool, got everybody's attention, and threw it in. When it finally disappeared, I shouted, "Come on," and ran across the road. Sure enough — there it came — surging out at an amazing speed. What a victory! They were astounded at my sagacity.

Life and death are like the whirlpool. All life is inevitably drawn in ever-increasing speed toward that all-consuming, spinning, whirling, central vortex — the center of the whirlpool — which sucks and pulls at us. We are like the frog — we struggle frantically for awhile, when we're young, strong, and feel invincible, but the whirlpool always wins — and what makes that bad is that we wonder where we go when we plunge into that tunnel — where it's all darkness and turbulence and unknown. Death frightens us, and although we get tired, like the frog, we keep struggling, until we just can't any more.

The mystery of death is created by the same problem my friends and I had. We simply don't see *the whole picture*. When we do, we see the other end of the culvert and realize that — "the stuff comes out on the other side."

I really wanted to jump into that whirlpool and swim through — I wasn't afraid anymore. I knew I could do it because *I saw the whole picture* and because I understood the *principle* of the whirlpool — that what goes in has to come out. You see, that is the law of whirlpools — they are *created* by the other end. If you block up the "exit end" of the culvert, you destroy the whirlpool. Life and death are like that. Death is not a bottomless pit — it's like the culvert, and every culvert has another opening, which is life. If there wasn't an outlet — there couldn't be an inlet. If death did not lead to life — there would be no death — or life, either.

And that's what the Bible is for — that's what Jesus came to do — to help us see *the whole picture* so that we don't wander around in a fog scared to death and wondering what life and death are all about. And that's why Christians don't have any fear of death —

because they *see the whole picture*
and they know that
"the stuff comes out on the other side."

Love Your Enemies

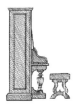

We had three teachers at Colerain school: Miss Smokey, Miss MacDonald, and Miss Rinault. I have no idea how it got the name Colerain. I guess it must not have been too important, because no one ever explained it to us. There was no office, no library, no principal, no gym, no cafeteria —

and no nonsense.

Miss Smokey was my teacher — she was beautiful, and I loved her. Russell Fanningsdorf came to our school in February 1944.

His mother marched him into our classroom — completely unannounced, one very cold, overcast morning — and placed him before Miss Smokey. Russell's mother was a portly, red-faced woman, dressed in a flowing, ankle-length, nondescript dress, a huge, thick, black sweater, and a babushka. You don't know the word *babushka,* do you? My goodness, what do they teach in school these days? A babushka is like a head scarf that ties under your chin. She would have made a classic portrait of a seventeenth-century peasant woman. She spoke almost no English. I understood only the word "school" and the name "Russell."

Our school was populated mainly by lower middle-class students, who consequently dressed very modestly. By comparison, Russell was dressed in rags —

and peculiar rags at that.

Russell didn't want to stay. He was obviously terrified. He cried and clung tenaciously to his mother. After communicating her desire to place Russell in our school, she turned and placed both of her hands on Russell's shoulders. I wish I could draw you a picture of that scene. It must have made a heavy impression upon me, because I can see them so clearly now — her round, rough, red face, worn by cares, old far before its time; her stubby, callused, work-hardened fingers, with the black dirt visible under the broken nails; her short, square body trembling —

she addressed him in German.

I will never know what she said, but Russell stopped crying, squared his shoulders, and accepted his fate. Finally, they separated, and Russell went to an unoccupied desk in the fourth-grade row. He sat all day in absolute silence, never acknowledging our stares or even our presence. He did not go out for recess or for lunch.

You must understand that it was 1944. Our country was engaged in a bitter conflict with Germany.

The Germans were our enemies.

Even as children, we had learned to hate, and there is no discrimination in a child's hatred. Russell was German. He spoke with a German accent. *We hated him.* We would not accept him; he was never one of us. He gradually – painfully – worked his way into the school routines, but he was a person apart. He was never chosen for a team, he was taunted, heckled, called *Kraut* and *Nazi* – we would imitate a German salute and say *Heil, Hitler* – he was abused in every way –

and he was alone.

He remained aloof. He did not cry; he did not respond or resist; he did not acknowledge us. *He had not a single friend, except Miss Smokey.* Her Herculean efforts to teach him, to reach him, to help him with his clothes, his speech – and to blast us with her withering looks and speeches for our cruelty – are an everlasting monument to her and to her kind. I thank God for Miss Smokey –

Russell's only friend.

To make matters even worse, the Fanningsdorfs had moved into an old abandoned farmhouse on Eighteen Mile Road, a place so run-down and rickety that no one had lived there for years, and there they raised pigs. Russell smelled of pig – and we reminded him of it.

Russell's life with us reached a climax late that spring. As you can easily imagine, he was a poor student. He barely spoke English, he never had paper or pencil, but always suffered the humiliation of having to borrow from Miss Smokey. He would not ask of us –

he knew the answer.

One bright, warm, spring day, Miss Smokey – in an attempt to rouse the interest of her flagging students – promised an afternoon holiday to our class if everyone scored a hundred on a spelling test. She obviously forgot about Russell. It wasn't a very hard test; I'm sure she meant for us to pass it. Even Russell might have, but he didn't. Whether he did it deliberately as a payback or whether he just didn't know, I can't guess. We graded each other's papers, and then read the scores out loud. Sure enough, Russell was the only one who missed a word, and we missed our holiday.

Now I come to the hard part of this story. How can I tell you this? What will you think of me? After school, two other boys (Doug Bussey and Tommy Petersen) and I jumped Russell and beat him up. I don't know what good we thought it would do. Even after forty years, the ache in my heart is almost unbearable.

Russell never came back to school that year, and I never saw him again until the following fall.

There are two lessons I wish to share with you. First, perhaps some of you who read this are teachers or plan to teach. *(Every parent is a teacher.* There is no more noble calling on this earth than to teach. Our Lord Jesus Christ was called "Teacher.") May God help you to be sensitive to the Russells who come to your schools – your classrooms. In a world of insensitivity, may they find in you some understanding – some sympathy – a friend.

Second, Christianity ought to make us better. I hope you can see what a negative reflection this incident was not only on me, but on my parents and the church where I attended. All the sermons, all the Sunday school lessons I had heard, all the examples I had seen did not teach me to *love my enemies.*

Oh, I had been taught the words,

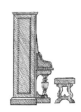

"You have heard that it was said,
'You shall love your neighbor,
and hate your enemy.'
But I say to you,
love your enemies,
and pray for those who persecute you."
—Matthew 5:43–44 NASB

I could quote that in my sleep, but I had not been taught the *application.* I did not see my attitude toward Russell as being a violation of anything I had been taught. My parents and their friends used racial slurs when speaking of Germans, Japanese, Chinese, "Negroes," and Italians. *It is no wonder my actions bothered me so little.*

Remember, parents, if there is an inconsistency between your behavior and your teaching – a child will nearly always copy your behavior.

Remember, also, that if our Christianity does not make us better in *practical situations,* it is useless to us.

God calls us to love our enemies –
it's no trouble to love our friends.

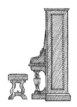

Marks

"Then the Lord put a mark on Cain
so that no one who found him would kill him."
—Genesis 4:15 NIV

I was looking at my hands this morning, and I noticed a small blue dot in the palm of my left one. Hands are amazing things, you know. It is interesting to me that most of my scars are on my left hand – it's because my left hand is nearly always holding the object my right hand is aiming at. I hold the hammer, the knife, the saw, or the screwdriver in my right hand, and I *operate* on whatever the left hand is holding. The scars are the result of missed communication between my hands. But the blue dot isn't.

It came from another source.

I have had that blue dot for over half a century. It was put there by a boy named Donny Hether (pronounced Hee'-ther). He sat right in front of me in the fifth grade. We weren't exactly friends, but then we certainly weren't exactly enemies, either. His folks owned a small grocery store right down John R. Road, not far from school. I realize that small, owner-operated grocery stores have mostly gone out of business – because now we are more interested in the price we pay than the people we buy from – but back then things were different, and the Hethers were sort of looked up to because everybody believed they *had money*. That sort of placed Donny in a different category from me.

Donny had nice clothes, and he got his hair cut pretty often by a real barber. He also had this stuff on his hair that made it look slick, and it smelled real sweet. Kids today would laugh at it, but then it was considered hot stuff. Donny would have been better off not to go to the barber's quite so often, because he had pretty big ears, and those close-cropped haircuts made them stand out.

Well, I was real bored in school one day – which happened altogether too often and led to most of my difficulties. The teacher was working with the sixth graders on some problem about the Russians getting half of Germany at the end of World War II, and I wasn't too interested – apparently neither was our government.

Anyway, I got to noticing Donny's right earlobe. It was because his head was right in front of my face, and from the rear, the most outstanding feature of Donny's head was his ears – and the most outstanding thing about his ears was his earlobes. Earlobes are a wonder – an absolute marvel. You know, they just sort of hang down there beside your head, kinda' soft and floppy and completely useless. I didn't know then that your earlobes are inherited or that some folks' earlobes are closely attached to their heads and other folks have earlobes that aren't –

Donny's weren't attached!

I could feel a powerful temptation sweeping over me to just reach up and flick his right earlobe and watch it jiggle. I fought it down several times because I really didn't have a reason – besides meanness – and I also had some notion that he might be sort of surprised and perhaps not take it as a friendly gesture. Well, the meanness got the best of me – which happened altogether too often – and I got my index finger locked real good behind my thumb, and I squeezed down until it fairly exploded. I thumped Donny's earlobe so hard that it flapped like a wet sheet hanging on a clothesline in a twenty-mile-an-hour wind.

Donny never yelped or moved. It was the most remarkable display of nerves and self-discipline I have ever seen. About thirty minutes later, he turned around. I had my left hand laying open – palm up on my desk – and he had this brand new, freshly sharpened yellow pencil – and he stuck it right in the palm of my hand. The lead broke off and stayed there – that's where the blue dot came from. He turned around and went right back to work.

You know, I never bothered Donny much after that.

The mark is still there, and I suspect that it's the only reason I remember Donny Hether. I have some other marks – some visible – some you can't see. They were put there by folks who touched my life in one way or another. I wonder how many folks are wandering around this earth with my marks on them? And –

I wonder what kind of marks they are?

Did you know that Scripture says that God put a mark on Cain, and it was one you could see. I have often wondered what it looked like. The apostle John tells us in Revelation that the redeemed have God's name written on their foreheads. I can't see it in the mirror, but that's one mark I'm glad

I have. I guess *we all leave marks of one kind or another on folks every day.* Maybe we ought to be more cautious, because sometimes –

even after fifty years,
that's how we're remembered.

The Light of Men

"In him was life,
and that life was the light of men.
The light shines in the darkness,
but the darkness has not understood it."
—John 1:4–5 NIV

When I was nine, they began the process of draining the swamp below our house. I was there every day – watching, climbing over the freshly unearthed dirt mounds, and getting in the way. I didn't know what their intentions were, so as they worked – digging the big, deep, drainage ditch – and laid the concrete pipe in the ditch, I was only fascinated by the size of the machinery and the excitement of the event. If I had known their intent, I'm sure I would have sabotaged the operation – because *I loved the swamp.*

It was the most fascinating thing in my world.

When they left, only the mounded ribbon of fresh dirt that covered the pipe remained as evidence of their passing. You know, a most peculiar thing happened, which has to do with the best laid plans of mice and men, I suppose. Their theory was to drain the swamp into a creek that ran about three or four hundred yards away. There was a rise in the ground, on top of which was the road to our house, which separated the north end of the swamp from the creek. Not long after they finished the drainpipe, we had several days of heavy rainfall. The creek flooded and the water ran from the creek, through the drain pipe, and poured into the swamp. Where it emptied into the swamp, the tremendous velocity of the rushing water dug out a huge hole, which later formed a large pond.

Swamp life migrated to this pond. Fish, leeches, turtles, muskrats, frogs – even ducks and geese – were found there in abundance. It became a favorite place. I often found myself wading and swimming in the pond, chasing something. Inevitably, I would always be drawn to the mouth of the drain pipe. It ran reasonably straight, and you could actually see through it – all the way to

> a tiny white *speck of light,*
> which winked and beckoned to me
> from the other end.

I entered the pipe on several occasions, but it was a *very tight fit,* and backing up was almost impossible – so after a few feet, I always squirmed back out. I suppose that considering my undauntable personality and insatiable curiosity, it was inevitable

> that I must try it.

One day my friend James MacFarland and I had been chasing a large turtle in the pond, but it eluded us by going into the drain pipe, which was just at water level. I went into the pipe to get the turtle, determined that it was not going to escape from me that easily. James followed me. I was so intent on capturing the turtle, that I had gone quite a ways, farther than ever before, before I realized that James was behind me. James was slightly larger than I, and when I stopped, he bumped into me.

"Did you get him?" he yelled. The muffled echo in those close quarters scared us.

"No," I whispered. "I guess he decided to just go on through. Let's go after him."

"No, let's go back," James urged, but when he tried to back up, he realized that he was stuck, and he panicked.

I wasn't exactly *happy,* but I mustered my most cheerful, reassuring voice and said, "Let's just crawl all the way through."

It took us about an hour, I think. In places the pipe was low, and collected water lay within four or five inches of the top – nasty, smelly, mucky water – water filled with leeches and crabs – water that had been laying there since the last rain. With heads pushing hard against the rough, concrete top of the drain pipe to keep the water out of our mouths and noses – we crawled on. We bloodied our knees and toes on the abrasive concrete, and the tops of our heads were scraped clean of either hair or skin. And of course, the turtle swam and crawled contentedly before us, completely oblivious to the circumstances. When we finally fell out the other end into the sunlight and fresh water of the creek — I was no longer concerned about the turtle —

I was just grateful to be alive.

Looking back, I reflect on what kept me going. Although I had my fearful moments, it was an exciting type of fear — like riding a roller coaster, I suppose. I can honestly say that I kept James going, and there were times that I even enjoyed the adventurous feeling I had. James knew we were going to die, that we would never be found, and he constantly despaired. For the whole time — the entire distance — he never turned loose of my ankle. Sometimes I look at my ankle even now, my left one to be exact, and I imagine that I can see the imprint of his desperately clutching fingers and the cuts he made with his fingernails. I whispered to him constantly of my confidence, my hope. "Not far now, James. We're almost there, James. We're going to make it, James. Don't worry, James."

Do you know what the difference was? Have you guessed my secret? Do you think I was braver, more adventurous, more determined? No — no, a thousand times *no!* The difference was that

I could see the light!

I could see the light! What a marvelous spiritual application that has! We live in a world of darkness, of dreary hopeless places that constantly threaten to suffocate us. There are voices that call us to quit, to see that it's hopeless — but then there is the light — the light that beckons us and invites us — the sweet light of hope and promise that is Jesus Himself. And the Light says —

"Not far now, John. Almost there, John.
Just a little more. You're going to make it.
Don't lose heart, John.
I'm with you, John."

Fear

It was March 31, 1944 or 1945. I remember the date because it was my birthday. Either my birthday fell on a Saturday that year or it was the Saturday after my birthday when this event took place. Traditionally, I always took my first swim of the year on my birthday. It wasn't a very old tradition, because I wasn't very old, but I had done it for two or three years in a row –

which to a child is an old tradition.

Even in years when spring came early, it was a real test of fortitude in Michigan. This year, spring was very late. The ice had only been gone for a week or so, and the deep, clear, blue-green spring water, which filled the abandoned gravel pit, was only slightly above freezing. It was a gray, overcast, windy, March day. We stood on the bank in our birthday suits – Tommy, Freddy, James and I – deliberating. We had huge chill bumps standing out all over our bodies, and we hadn't even gotten wet yet. We looked at each other, each one hoping that somebody would say, "I'm putting my clothes back on and going home; this is stupid." But we were just boys, and we still believed that *displaying strength* was greater than *showing wisdom.*

"It's *your* birthday," James stated; "you should go in first" – to which Tommy and Freddy both immediately assented. It made perfectly good sense, but I hated it. "You guys are just chicken," I retorted, "but I'm going to go." As soon as the words were out of my mouth, I deeply regretted them, because now there was nothing else for me to *say* – it was time to *do* – and so I did. Tommy and Freddy were right behind me, but James stayed on the bank and put his clothes back on. *James was the intellectual in our group.* Tommy changed his mind almost as soon as he hit the water and went back to shore. Tommy was only slightly less intelligent than James. Freddy and I kept going. I'm not too sure what that says about our intelligence level –

but I am sure it isn't complimentary.

Our objective was an island in the center of the gravel pit. It wasn't far – thirty yards maybe – but I would never have made it. I simply grew so numb with cold that I had no control over my arms and legs. Freddy was two years older than I – much stronger and a better swimmer – he grabbed me and pulled me to the shore. It was not a case of *maybe,* it simply was a fact that I would have drowned without him.

Memories
of Clark
Road

◆

227

Now I was faced with a terrible dilemma. I was on the island, the cold wind on my wet, naked body was unbearable, and there was only one way back –

the same way that I got there –
swimming.

James said he would go and get my dad, but it didn't take long to decide that drowning was by far the better of those two evils. I was not long making up my mind. I dove in and thrashed my way furiously and blindly to shore as if a demon were after me. I even outdistanced Freddy. I was shocked when my outstretched hands began grabbing gravel, and I guess I was six feet up the bank before I quit trying to swim. I dressed as quickly as possible and headed for home.

A person rarely performs at his capacity unless there is *appropriate motivation*. That is as true of adults as children. I have been motivated by anger, by reason, and by love. In this case, I was motivated by *fear*. It was fear of being thought a coward that made me jump in. It was fear of discovery, fear of dying, and fear of what that meant that made me keep going. Let there be no doubt that God not only knows the power of fear, but has consistently used it to produce the desired results in His children. Appropriate use of fear is a valuable tool in child rearing. The divine stamp of approval has been placed upon it. *Any parents who mistakenly refrain from motivating their children through this medium severely handicap their potential for successful child rearing.*

Let me caution you to think about the word *appropriate* – fear motivation must never be an excuse for bullying or cruelty. God is a God of balance – of propriety – and He would have us imitate His wisdom.

The Other Side of Fear

I was eight that summer – the summer of forty-five – so were James, Tommy, and Doug. It was another turning point in my life, although I didn't know anything about turning points and I certainly didn't mean for it to be.

I had much simpler things in mind.

The great war ended that summer, and our brothers, husbands, uncles, fathers, and sons came home – at least many of them did. The dark cloud of war passed away, and a state of great exuberance, hope, and lightheartedness seemed to settle over the country. Everybody was happy and carefree, people laughed more and sang more. The weather was great, the gardens were producing a bumper crop, the lyrics to popular music became brighter, people were getting married in droves, even the sermons at church seemed to be less somber and threatening. School was out, and I had three months of nothing ahead of me but swimming, fishing, baseball, and roaming the countryside.

What a time to be alive.

The Salt Water Swimming Pool was right down the hill from our house. Looking back, it seems very strange that there should be a swimming pool near us, because we lived in a very sparsely settled, rural area. How it got there and why it was there still puzzles me – but it was there – right on the corner of Clark Road and Rochester Road.

It cost a quarter to get in. I never had one, but the people who owned it were very understanding and would let me do odd jobs for the price of admission. I started going there when I was five, I think. It had two diving boards, one about three feet off the water and one about twelve. The first year I went, I watched with envy and admiration as the older boys strode with measured, rhythmic steps to the end of the diving boards, jumped high, pushed down hard, and allowed the spring of the boards to propel them high into the air as they dove gracefully into the water. I walked out on the three-foot board in 1943, when I was six. I remember the growing fear, the queasiness in my stomach, as I gingerly edged my way to the end. When I looked down, the water was unbelievably far away. I closed my eyes and jumped – shocked at how soon I hit the water. Before the summer was over, I was jumping and diving regularly and fearlessly, and I began to look apprehensively at the twelve-foot board.

The next summer, when I was seven, my friends and I made a pact that we would conquer the twelve-foot board. I was the first to try it. I walked out slowly – careful to stay in the middle lest I fall off – and I looked down. The distance to the water was staggering. I stood long at the end of the board, my friends taunting me, but the dizzying nausea in my stomach made my legs weak and broke my will. I was absolutely frozen with fear, and gently, ever so slowly, I placed one foot behind the other and retreated to the safety of the platform. Several days passed, and all of my friends succeeded,

before I tried it again. Once again, by the end of summer, it was a regular thing.

There was another board.

It wasn't a diving board, really, and you are going to have to use your imagination to see this — and you really must see it to appreciate it. An iron pipe about four inches in diameter had been sunk into the concrete immediately in front of the platforms that supported the diving boards. It was attached, for stability, to the platforms at both levels, and it rose some ten or fifteen feet above the twelve-foot platform. Iron rungs, so small in diameter that they hurt your feet, had been welded to the pipe — beginning at the twelve-foot level. At the top of the iron pipe was a socket into which was placed a flagpole, and attached to the pipe, right at the socket, was a small platform — about eight inches wide and two feet long. During the summer of forty-five, Tommy, Doug, James, and I vowed we would dive from that platform.

I went up the ladder twice, early that summer, to insert the flagpole into its place. Going up was relatively easy, because the tendency is to fix your eyes on your destination and you don't have to look down or feel for the rungs —

like you do on the way down.

Once the flag was in place, I would first look around — amazed at what I could see from my vantage point. Then my eyes would be drawn down — down to the water. That sick, nauseous feeling and the frightening dizziness would come, causing me to cling to the ladder desperately. I would close my eyes — establish my equilibrium — and very slowly begin searching for the next lowest rung, and then the next, knowing that I must not open my eyes until I felt the wooden platform.

Tommy tried it first. It was July. He made it to the top of the ladder all right, but he had to be pried loose by the lifeguard, because he got so scared he wouldn't release his grip. His pleas for help caused all of us to be very sober. Two weeks later, Doug tried it; he did better. He made it to the top of the ladder, but the pipe ended at the flagpole socket, so you had to hold on to the flagpole itself as you climbed the last three rungs — and the flagpole wasn't very steady with the wind pulling the flag and bending the pole. Balancing was very tricky. Doug tried to crawl onto the platform on his hands and knees, but it was too small. In the process —

he lost his nerve and nearly fell.

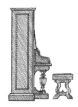

August came and time grew short – the summer of forty-five was almost at an end. Doug moved away in the middle of August, and we never saw him again – it took some of the spirit out of our resolve. Every day I would stand and look up at the flagpole. The joy of the other boards was greatly diminished, and the pool wasn't as much fun as it had been. One morning it rained, but early in the afternoon the sun came out for a short time. I went to the pool alone. I knew what I was going to do. I practiced climbing the ladder. I must have gone up and down twenty times or more. I was determined to conquer my fear of the ladder. Finally, I was able to rest at the top – and even look down – without getting sick and dizzy. I made a plan for how to get out on the board – I memorized every hand hold and movement. I knew I must do it quickly – I must never hesitate, never consider what could go wrong – and once on the board, I must dive immediately.

That night I prayed much about it, and the next day I did it. I did it just like I had planned. I stepped out on the board, closed my eyes, and without hesitation – I dove.

It seemed an eternity before I hit the water.

Words will fail me here. It is truly amazing how many sensations can be experienced in so brief a moment – the acceleration as I sliced through the air on the way to the water – the incredible jolt as I hit the water – my hands slamming into the bottom of the pool, almost immediately – bursting to the surface – swimming leisurely to the steps – being congratulated by my friends – and then standing there looking at that platform where I had just been. It was overwhelming – too much, too quickly. Fear, excitement, joy, satisfaction, relief, pride, exultation – they were all mine in a few seconds. I think I know how David felt when he walked out to face Goliath – when he saw that stone find its mark and Goliath drop to the ground dead. I knew what feelings must have gone through his mind, as the entire Israelite army cheered and the Philistines ran.

It was amazing how different that platform looked

from the other side.

Very few times in all my years have I experienced that type of complete satisfaction. I was on *the other side of fear,* the affirmative side – the side you can only know about if you have the faith to pass through fear. Those whose *unbelief* causes them to back away from fear on the front side only know fear as a *deterrent* – only experience the nausea, the dizziness, the paralyzing, terrifying frustration of defeat.

I have been afraid many times since the summer of forty-five. I have experienced all of its effects – down to the sweaty palms – but I believe that the summer of forty-five established a precedent for moving through fear. Just as fear builds and increases if we respond negatively to it, so those who pass through – those who experience the other side of fear – the positive side – are those for whom fear becomes an incentive. They still experience the *symptoms* of fear, but those very symptoms become a source of motivation – because they anticipate the other side.

The summer of forty-five –
The other side of fear.
No one can take you through it.
You must climb the ladder alone –
take the dive alone.
And you must do it by faith.

I Got Away with It

My gun case contains a wide variety of weapons. Some of them are quite expensive and carefully made. But there is one there that is neither expensive nor well made, but it never fails to attract attention. When people ask, "What's that?" I tell them that it is a model 42 Winchester pump .22 and that it is a "special" gun. I'm sure they notice the solemnity and reverence with which I pick it up. The bluing is completely gone and the stock has been broken in two and is held together with two brass machine screws. The barrel has a swollen place, because it was fired one time with an obstruction in it. My father traded Elmer Russell a .38-caliber pistol for it in 1943. He told me it was to be mine, but he kept it in his room. Sometimes in the late summer evenings or on Sunday afternoons, he would take it out and we would shoot tin cans.

I don't think he ever *specifically* told me that I was not to take it out when he was not there, but it was another of those things that I knew. One Saturday, my folks went somewhere and my sister was gone to a girlfriend's house

– they either took her or she walked – anyway, I was at home alone. What made me think of the gun was finding a loaded .22-shell at a sort of local dump, not too far from our house. I put it in my pocket, but –

it seemed to burn a hole there.

When I got home, thoughts of that gun completely occupied my mind. *I knew better,* but I simply could not, or would not, overcome the urge to get it. I believe the determining factor was the thought that –

"Nobody will ever know."

Somehow, that gave me confidence to proceed. I convinced myself that it couldn't be wrong if nobody found out. I got the gun, loaded it, and began looking for a target. I only had one shell, so I had to be selective. I wanted to shoot a bird, but my father's stern warnings about firing it in the air carried too much weight – I had visions of breaking a window two miles away and getting caught. Ultimately, I shot a tin can by the chicken coop – it was very unrewarding. An unloaded gun is not much fun, so I hastily put it away.

I don't think my folks ever found out. At least, it was never mentioned – and I'm sure that means they never knew. I guess you could say "I got away with it" – but I didn't. For days – weeks – afterward, I lived in mortal fear that my father would somehow discover my disobedience. And it wasn't just that, either; I felt lousy about what I had done. I felt as if I had betrayed my father – as if I were lying to him every day. And I still haven't gotten away with it.

Every time I look at that gun,
I remember.

My father always meant for me to have the gun and to enjoy it. But he wanted me to enjoy it *on terms that were best for me.* The gift had great potential for me *if used properly* – and according to his instructions.

I haven't changed much; it's just that my *heavenly* Father's gifts to me have grown much more expensive, and they have far greater possibilities for my enjoyment and fulfillment. Sometimes I abuse them – I use them indiscriminately and for purposes for which they were not intended. I still try to convince myself that I can – "get away with it" – and that if it is not known, there can be no harm. It is not so. The tragedy is that when I use His gifts contrary to their purpose and His intentions, they become a curse to me – a source of guilt and depression.

Perhaps the highest praise to God's name, the most sincere thanksgiving for His gracious bounty, and the deepest communion between God and man is realized in

the appropriate use of all of His gifts.

God and the Nickel

When I was a boy, "pop" was only a nickel. In other places, they called it "Coke" – even if it wasn't – or "soda" – but we always called it "pop," and it was only a nickel. I know it's hard to believe, but unless you understand that, you won't get much out of this story. Nickels were hard to come by – that's why pop was a nickel – something about economics and the law of supply and demand. Anyway, there was this Standard Oil Station on the corner of Eighteen Mile Road and Rochester Road, which was about a half mile from my house. It was owned by a guy named Marshall Bruder, which isn't too important, but it's neat to know if you're into that sort of thing.

Well, Marshall Bruder sold candy out of a glass case, and he had a red pop machine with "Coca Cola" written in white cursive letters on the side. It was one of those old kinds of machines that had ice – and real cold water – in the bottom, and the bottles of pop sat right down in the water – *that's what made them cold,* in case you're a little slow on the uptake, and that's also what made them so desirable – the pop, I mean. You don't ever see ads saying –

"Get your room-temperature pop right here."

On real hot days in the summertime, I used to go to Marshall Bruder's with Tommy and Freddy Petersen. We used to go to Marshall Bruder's Standard Oil Station because the concrete floors inside were so smooth and cool on our bare feet and because we would open the lid of the pop machine and stick our hands way down deep – up to our elbows – in that ice cold water. It was delicious. Mrs. Bruder would eventually run us out. Not too quickly, though – and she wasn't mean or anything. When we left, we'd get a drink out of their artesian well. The water was cold and sweet. They had this rock wall all around the well, and it formed a sort of pool – very small, but it was a neat place to play.

I want to get back to the pop machine, though. Every time I opened that lid, I would think about how neat it would be to say, "Gimme a pop" – just like my dad or other grown-ups who came into Marshall Bruder's. "Gimme a pop." I used to practice saying it when I was alone – I'd walk down Clark Road saying, "Gimme a pop" – I'd walk around the house saying, "Gimme a pop." My mother would say, "What did you say?" and I'd say – "Oh nothin'." They had Coca Cola, but they also had R.C. Cola, Byerly's Grape – and Nesbitt's Orange. That was what I really wanted. I had it all figured out. When Mr. Bruder would say, "What kind of pop?" I'd say, "Nesbitt's Orange." But, I never had a nickel – neither did Tommy or Freddy. Things grow in a child's mind – they get out of proportion, and that's what led me to do

something unthinkable.

We went to this real small church that met in a Masonic Lodge in Hazel Park, Michigan. My dad led singing; another guy – Bob Winegar – did too, but my dad was the *real* song leader. Brother Utley was the preacher. It was a real good church. I liked going to church there because Brother Utley was a soft-spoken, kindly sort of man who talked to the kids like they were people, and he got the boys up in front and asked us Bible questions and taught us to lead singing, and he never yelled or scared me. When my dad led singing, he made me want to sing because he so obviously enjoyed himself.

After communion, they took up the collection. It was sort of confusing to me, because when they took up the collection, they always said it was "separate and apart" from the Lord's Supper –

but even a child could see that it wasn't.

The money went in these wicker baskets with green velvet bottoms. The bottoms were soft like that, so you wouldn't be embarrassed when you dropped change in the basket. I figured that out by myself. When it was all collected, they put the baskets with the money up front under the communion table. I don't know if the idea seized me all at once or if it crept over me very subtly and slowly. I only know that one Sunday after church – while everybody was outside visiting because it was so hot inside – I went back inside, walked right up to the communion table, and took a nickel out of the collection plate. I guess I thought that God wouldn't mind losing a lousy nickel for a bottle of pop – I mean – what's a nickel to God. It's very important that you understand that I could have taken anything – a five dollar bill, even. But I didn't want a five dollar bill –

I wanted a nickel – wanted one so badly
that I risked going to hell to get it.

Nobody ever knew. I put it in my pocket, and the next day when Tommy, Freddy, and I went to Marshall Bruder's, I had it with me. But when the time came to say, "Gimme a pop," I couldn't do it – I mean, the words just wouldn't come out, and it scared me because I would try to say the words and I couldn't. I tried it again the next day, and it was worse, so I put the

nickel in a shoe under my bed, and I didn't touch it again. But it haunted me. I couldn't get that nickel out of my mind. I couldn't sleep, and when I did I had terrible dreams. God would speak to me; He would say in a very loud voice –

"Where is My nickel? – I want My nickel."

God was so *real* to me – so incredibly, practically *real,* and I realized I had done a terrible thing – committed a sin beyond reckoning. I had stolen money right out of God's very own pocket –

and I was terrified.

I couldn't wait for the next Sunday to come – I was so anxious to get to church that I was in a sweat. I prayed that God would just let me live long enough to put that nickel in the collection tray when it was passed, so the nightmare would be over and I would know that I was forgiven.

Sunday came. When we got to church, I couldn't sing – somehow it didn't seem right – and I didn't hear anything Brother Utley said. All I could think about was that nickel in my pocket – and *here I was, right in God's very presence,* and anything could happen. Brother Utley might stop any moment and say, "We have a thief in our midst," and every eye would turn toward me, because somehow they would know. They might prove who stole it by casting lots – like they did with Achan – I always figured it was sort of like a game we played called "Odd Man Out" – and I knew that I would get the short stick and they would stone me to death.

My mother had given me a coin to put in the collection tray, but as it came, I found it impossible to put the extra nickel in without detection, because we sat up front and there wasn't anything else in the basket.

My plan was foiled.

After church, everybody went outside just like the week before. I crept very carefully back in, but this time with much *fear and reverence.* Like a Jew approaching the Ark of the Covenant, I approached the communion table. I was trembling from head to foot – absolutely terror stricken. I bent over and prayed a little prayer, "God, please forgive me for stealing this nickel. I promise I'll never do it again. In Jesus name, Amen." I placed the nickel, very gently, back into the collection tray and ran out of the building as rapidly as I could.

I was so happy, so relieved, so forgiven. No prisoner ever experienced a greater thrill of freedom and forgiveness. God had graciously made it possible for me to come back into His presence. I felt so good that I sang church songs in the backseat of the car on the way home.

But somewhere along the way, I lost some of that childlike faith in God's real presence, with the awe and reverence it brought. Somehow, I have grown to believe that *God is not concerned with the nickels I steal from Him,* and I no longer tremble with fear at His displeasure. Somehow, I have developed an almost casual and relaxed attitude toward the gathering of the saints – and I do not hasten anxiously into His presence with cries of penitence – and I have less sense of joy in forgiveness.

O God, restore unto me the joy of your salvation;
Renew my sense of Your divine presence;
Help me to understand my sinfulness.
May I once again rejoice in the Cross of Jesus,
and may I never again take for granted
the grace You have bestowed.
May I be so overwhelmed by your faithfulness
that I sing with gladness your praises
and shout the majesty of your name.
May your presence be so real that
I fall to my knees and cry,
"Holy, Holy – Holy is the Lord of Hosts."

Value

On Clark Road we had a grape arbor. Huge clusters of dark, purple, Concord grapes grew there. I was nuts about them (maybe I should say *grapes* about them). As soon as they were ripe – and sometimes before – I would pull a whole cluster and pinch the thin skins between my thumb and forefinger, squeezing the purple juice and greenish pulpy mass inside my mouth. I got so good at it that I could do a grape about every two seconds. But no matter how hard I tried, I couldn't even make a dent in the overall population of grapes. I would leave huge piles of skins where I had stood –

but the vines looked untouched.

Before the first frost, my mom and I would make grape juice. We'd gather bushels of grapes – pull them from the stems, wash them, sort them – getting out the unripe and the rotten – and then we'd put them in cheese cloth and crush them, collecting the beautiful, dark, clear juice in a huge pan. My memory fails me on some parts of the process from that point. I know we dipped the "Ball Jars" – which we had saved from last year – in boiling water. Then we poured in the juice, poured a layer of paraffin wax on top, put on a seal, and screwed on the lid – my dad always did that part because he could get it tighter than anyone else. We made quite a bit, and it was very good. We kept it in the fruit cellar under the house.

During the winter and into the spring, we would open a jar occasionally. My mother was very frugal by nature, and she rationed the grape juice out to us in what seemed thimblefuls – every mouthful was treasured. There was no swilling it down in huge gulps; so a small glass was sipped carefully, lasting all evening.

Grape juice was *valuable* stuff.

I suppose it wasn't particularly good grape juice by today's standards. We didn't strain it as well as we would have liked, so there was a lot of sediment at the bottom. I could never get the paraffin sealer out cleanly, so pieces of wax were always floating in it. My mother put very little sugar in it – couldn't afford that – so some of it was quite bitter. Invariably, toward spring, some of it would begin to ferment – due to a hole in the paraffin or a lid not sealed properly –

we drank it anyway.

It was the highlight of every holiday, birthday, or occasion, and I felt like royalty every time I was sent to the cellar to get a jar. It seemed an eternity between the last of it and the new crop.

What made me think about making grape juice is that I just returned from the refrigerator. Inside is a half-gallon plastic container filled with "Welch's" – well, it *was* filled; it's about half-empty now. This grape juice comes frozen in a can, it has no sediment, it is absolutely uniform in taste, there are never pieces of paraffin in it, and it never ferments. There is no picking, sorting, crushing, or boiling – you just add water. I just drained a sixteen-ounce glass in two draughts. I hardly noticed the taste. It cost me almost nothing. I do not fear running out. Our freezer has several cans.

I pay no attention.

It's an old story, a lesson told and retold by succeeding generations of parents and teachers from the beginning of time. Its truth is ageless and bottomless. I never learn it so completely that the next time it washes over me I do not feel it fresh – the lesson of *value*. What makes things have worth?

It is always what I pay –
what it costs –
how much suffering
or love goes into it!

A thing's value is in direct proportion to how much of myself I have invested in it.

⅌

A Christmas Memory

"Then Jesus told his disciples a parable
to show them that they should always pray
and not give up."
—Luke 18:1 NIV

In 1946 we had Christmas dinner at Aunt Velma's. I was nine. Aunt Velma was my mother's youngest sister. She was married to my uncle Brett Snoddy – pronounced, *Snow'-dee*. They were always pretty touchy about their last name, so I want to make sure I don't offend them – though I haven't seen any of them for thirty years, at least.

Aunt Velma had five children – Brett Jr., Bobby, Sidney, Nancy, and David. David was my age, and Nancy was my sister's age. Brett Jr. and Bobby were much older than I.

In 1946 the Snoddys were living in a log house – it had an open ceiling with big log support beams – it was a fascinating place. Anyway, Brett Jr. and Bobby had been drafted, because of the war, and I had not seen them in a long time – but now the war was over, and they were going to be home for Christmas.

We got there pretty early, and we opened presents. Brett Jr. was there when we got there, but Bobby wasn't, and I could tell that Aunt Velma was upset about it. I heard her tell my mom that Bobby had called and said he was trying to hitchhike because he didn't have money for a bus.

The day went by pretty quickly for me – we built a huge and elaborate snowman – complete with a carrot nose, charcoal eyes and ears, and a top hat and scarf. Then we had a snowball fight, after which we went ice skating on the creek that ran near their house. By dinnertime, I was famished. Aunt Velma postponed dinner as long as she could – but Bobby didn't show. Finally, we sat down to eat without him. Aunt Velma set a place for Bobby, and she put a chair for him at the table. I think it sort of made everybody solemn –

looking at that empty chair.

The Snoddy's weren't religious people, and usually they just dove right into whatever was on the table, but today Aunt Velma asked my dad to pray. It took her a minute or two to get it out, but she asked my dad to pray that God would take care of her Bobby and send him home. Her voice was all shaky and choked up, and when I looked at her, I saw that she was crying – the tears were running down her cheeks and

dripping right into her plate.

Everybody got real sad. We all bowed our heads, but for some reason, my dad didn't get right into his prayer, and when he did, it was a lot different from the one he usually prayed – the one I could say by heart. When he finished, it was pretty quiet for awhile – but then we started passing things and eating and talking, and everybody sort of got loosened up – like you always do – and we laughed and told stories. Even Aunt Velma joined in. It was a great dinner.

We were eating dessert when it happened – I mean we had totally forgotten –

but He hadn't.

One of the boys said, "Somebody just pulled into the driveway," and everything stopped, but nobody moved. Then a car door slammed, and there was a knock on the door. It's funny how you react to things. Everybody just sat and looked at each other – everybody but Aunt Velma. She was already up serving dessert.

"It's Bobby," she cried, "God has sent Bobby home; I just know He has."

"Now Velma, don't get your hopes up," Uncle Brett said. "It's probably someone else."

Now everybody started to get up, but nobody could beat Aunt Velma to the door. She was determined that it was Bobby –

and it was.

I don't know what anybody else thought, because we didn't talk about it, but I never doubted for one minute that God had sent Bobby home –

and I still don't doubt it.

I was nine. Sometimes I think those marvelous events were just for me –

For me to remember,
when I have doubts.
For me to tell you about,
when you have doubts.

The Kingdom of Heaven

"The kingdom of heaven
is like a merchant seeking fine pearls,
and upon finding one pearl of great value,
he went and sold all that he had,
and bought it."
—Matthew 13:46 NASB

Marbles was the game we played. There was no basket or ball for basketball, no one owned a football, baseball took too much time for recess or lunch hour – so we played marbles. We drew circles about five feet in diameter in the dirt, and everyone contributed a prearranged number of marbles to go inside the circle – which we called "the pot." We played for keeps. If you hit a marble with your shooter and knocked it outside the line that marked the pot, it was yours. There were rules against *hunching, eyedroppers,* and *throwing.*

There were three basic kinds of marbles – *aggies, steelies,* and *peries.* Everybody had a favorite shooter, a special marble prized above all the others. Mine was a perfect peri. I do not know the derivation of that word, and I spelled it *by ear.* I only know that we used it to signify a marble that was above average in size, perfectly clear, and perfectly round. There were only two or three in the entire school, so a peri was considered quite a prize.

My teacher, Miss Smokey, allowed marbles on the playground, marbles in the pockets, and marbles in your desk; but any marble in her classroom that became *visible* – was hers. She collected hundreds during the course of the year. A boy, who had suffered some severe losses to my peri and who was extremely envious, persuaded me to show it to him in the boy's bathroom. When I produced it, he slapped it out of my hand and ran to Miss Smokey. She took it. I mourned the loss of my shooter like a lost friend.

Since Miss Smokey had no use for marbles, she had devised a fascinating way of giving them back. Late in the spring, she would take her hoard of marbles and place it in a box on top of her desk. She had the boys line up behind the desk (girls did not play marbles in our school), and then she would tip over the box, and we would scramble after them.

I lined up in a very advantageous position, having remembered where most of the marbles went the previous year, and consequently seized upward of a hundred marbles –

but not the one I wanted.

It was found by a third grader. I offered him a penny for it, but he declined. I offered to bust his head if he didn't give it to me, but he declined that offer also – and since he had an eighth-grade brother, I didn't push the issue. I was determined to get my shooter, and I finally asked what he would take for it. He said that he would trade me the peri for the hundred marbles I had captured.

It wasn't hard.

I mean, I never hesitated. He could have asked for every marble I owned, and I would gladly have given them to him. I was so glad to get my shooter back that I thought I had made the best deal of my life. All those other marbles meant nothing to me. I carried my shooter home, stopping along the way to take it out of my pocket and hold it up to the sunlight to admire its flawless perfection –

and I was happy.

Memories
of Clark
Road

♦

244

I wish I could say I still have that marble. Along with kites, toy trucks, and "ring around the rosy," my fervor for them faded with age, and marbles no longer occupied my thoughts. My shooter passed quietly out of my life. I have my memories, and I remember how totally happy I was — absolutely satisfied — with my trade. Today, I know how that pearl merchant Jesus talked about felt, and I know that

the *kingdom* of heaven
is my pearl of great price.

I also understand that I have to sacrifice all of my "marbles" to have it. Maybe the reason I am often unhappy in my quest for that great pearl is that I see what I'm trading as having value, and I'm reluctant to give up so much of *certain* value for something of *uncertain* value.

❧

Home

When I left 736 Clark Road in 1947, it was the only *home* I had ever known. I was ten. I fought the move with every ounce of my being. I left everything I knew — all that was familiar.

My father could never find a resting place after that, and so between the ages of ten and seventeen, we wandered from house to house, from town to town, job to job — looking — looking for something that he could not define, but thought he would know if he saw. I guess he never saw it — or at least he never recognized it — so he died still looking. I could always tell when it was moving time — the discontent — the restlessness — bills piling up — the job wasn't working out. It was time to move again. During those years, I only knew that *home* was wherever Mom and Dad were, but I had no physical notion of home.

Home was just another temporary stopping place.

Memories of Clark Road

♦

246

After I graduated from high school, I went to Tennessee to go to college. While I was there, Michigan – in some general sense – became home. If anybody asked me where I was from or where my *home* was, I said, "Michigan." My family lived there, and I spent summers and holidays there. My sister and brother-in-law moved to Flint, Michigan, in 1956, and they lived there about twenty-five years. Her home became home to me. That's where I spent birthdays and holidays. It's where I went when I was troubled or lonely.

After twenty-five years, they left Michigan and moved to Georgia. Their move left me with a feeling of loneliness and emptiness. Mom and Dad were both dead. There was no reason to ever go back to Michigan. I have nothing there but memories.

Michigan is not *home* anymore.

Some years ago, I went back to the place on Clark Road – to show my children where I was raised. The old house was there, but it was much altered. The grape arbor was gone, and the huge pear tree – which had served as a ship, plane, and tank and had carried me on hundreds of adventures – was gone also. The trees had grown, the chicken coop – into whose wall I smashed my sister's brand new bicycle – was gone. They had even changed the name of the road from "Clark" to "Creston." Now why would they want to do that? How can a person find *home,* if they change everything?

The swamp below our house, where I turned Pete Vincent's hogs loose, has been drained, and strange people have built houses there – people who neither know nor care that their house is sitting on *my* swamp. They know nothing of me or Pete Vincent's hogs or the marvelous shot my father made, killing a cock pheasant there one winter evening when the swamp was frozen. You see, it was an easy shot at first, but my father's hands were so numb from the cold that he couldn't get the safety off on his gun, and the bird was out of range when he finally fired. I watched it sail, with its wings set, all the way to Eighteen Mile Road before it went down. I was sad that he had missed, but he told me he was sure he had hit the bird. I wanted badly to believe him. We walked all the way across the swamp in the gathering darkness, the freezing wind blowing fine flakes of new snow around us. Our dog, Betty, found the bird dead in a clump of marsh grass and cattails.

My father allowed me to carry the gun on the way home, and I walked close to him, knowing that surely no boy had as fine a father as I.

But, the swamp is gone,
and so is my father.

During the intervening years, I have followed my father's pattern – moving from house to house, town to town, job to job. I always knew that I was looking for something. I didn't know exactly what it was, but I knew I would know it if I saw it. I have never seen it, and now I know why. *It is not here!* I am not going to *find it* – it will *find me.* When I cross the Great River and open my eyes on the other side, I will know that this is it – that I am finally and forever home – that every tree, every building, every rock and blade of grass is exactly where it ought to be – where I always knew it would be – and I will say,

> "Why, here it is –
> yes, this is it exactly.
> How foolish I have been."

As Christians – and as parents – we must help our children to develop a strong sense of *home.* While it is true that on this earth we are pilgrims and strangers, it is also true that heaven is our "eternal home." That is why Jesus talked about there being "many mansions" in His Father's house. It was God's eternal plan to create powerful, internal feelings through the physical home, in order to generate those same longings for our permanent place of rest –

our *heavenly home.*

Parents have no greater obligation than to create a home atmosphere that makes their children's ideas of heaven take on real and specific meaning.

I hope you're excited about going *home.* I hope your enthusiasm is growing in anticipation of arriving – of being reunited – of being where you *belong.* Heaven, like *home,* is where your family is. It's where you'll spend your birthdays and holidays for the next million years or so.